1.0   Introduction

The recent increases in the price of gasoline have focused attention on all levels of the gasoline supply chain, from refining to retail. Following Hurricane Katrina retail prices jumped more than 50 cents per gallon over several days in some cities, leading to claims of 'gouging'. In response to these price spikes the U.S. Congress considered legislation providing civil and criminal sanctions for price gouging.[1] In contrast, states have expressed concern about new retail formats (primarily supermarkets and mass merchandisers) selling gasoline at too *low* a price. In response to these concerns, some states have modified or increased enforcement of "sales below cost" or *minimum* markups laws.[2]

The increased concern about gasoline pricing has led to increased interest in how retail gasoline prices are determined and how they change. Previously, large panel data sets of station specific gasoline prices have generally not been available. Recently, credit card (i.e., "fleet card") transaction data has enabled researchers to examine the pricing behavior of a large number of gasoline stations over an extended period of time.

We use a three year panel data set of weekly gasoline prices based on fleet card transactions from 272 gasoline stations located in the Northern Virginia suburbs of Washington, DC, along with a census of the stations in the area (consisting of station locations and a wealth of station characteristics), to establish a number of new empirical findings about retail gasoline pricing and relate these findings to the existing theoretical literature on pricing behavior. Our analysis suggests deficiencies in existing theories in explaining retail gasoline pricing.

Our first finding is that the retail markup (defined as retail price less a measure of wholesale price and taxes) for gasoline shows sizeable changes over time and these changes are persistent. In other words, there are sizeable regime changes in average margins. For

---

[1] Many states have gouging statutes. Following Hurricane Katrina more than 100 gasoline stations were investigated by states for gouging. See: Federal Trade Commission (2006).

[2] At least six states (Alabama, Kansas, New York, Michigan, Virginia, and Wisconsin) have considered legislation that would have introduced or modified minimum markup or sales below costs laws on gasoline. See FTC staff letter to The Honorable Gene DeRossett, Michigan House of Representatives, June 2004.

http://www.ftc.gov/os/2004/06/040618staffcommentsmichiganpetrol.pdf

instance, in our sample, the weekly median margin is more than 17 cents per gallon for 26 consecutive weeks (the mean of the median is 19.4 cents) in 1997 and 1998 before falling to less than 14 cents a week (the mean of the median is 10.7 cents) for 12 weeks. While the changing margins may be partially explained by asymmetric price adjustment, our empirical work suggests that equilibrium margins are changing as well.

Second, we find that stations do not appear to use simple static pricing rules: stations do not charge a fixed mark-up over their wholesale costs, nor do they maintain their relative position in the pricing distribution over time. Instead, a particular gasoline station frequently changes its relative position in the pricing distribution, sometimes dramatically. From one week to the next, stations are more likely than not to change their relative position measured in either dollars (above or below the regional mean) or rank (price relative to closest stations).[3] There is, however, heterogeneity in station's pricing decisions. Stations that charge very high or very low prices in one period are much more likely to charge high or low prices in subsequent periods. Interestingly, there appears to be an asymmetry in this behavior. Stations charging low prices appear to remain low priced stations for much longer periods than high priced stations. Surprisingly, while some stations consistently charge relatively high or low prices, the only station characteristic that is a good predictor of this heterogeneity is a station's brand affiliation. Other stations characteristics, e.g., offering repair services or full service gasoline, and measures of localized competition are not consistently associated with a station's retail mark-up.

Third, while there is heterogeneity in gasoline station pricing, with some stations charging, on average, high or low prices, a subset of gasoline stations change their average pricing strategy over time. Roughly 30% of stations significantly change their "typical price" (defined as a station's mean price in a year relative to the mean price in Northern Virginia in that year) from one year to the next. Between 1997 and 1998 nearly 25% of gasoline stations changed their relative position in the pricing distribution by more than 20 percentile points, e.g., moving from the 70th percentile to the 50th percentile. The observed changes in pricing strategy are economically important. During our sample period, the mean station earned a margin of roughly 14 cents a gallon. Between 1997 and 1998, 33% of stations changed their *relative* margin by roughly 4 cents. This corresponds to a change in retail mark-up roughly

---

[3] Lach (2002) finds very similar results in a sample of retail prices of consumer goods in Israel; i.e., the relative position of a retailer in the pricing distribution changes frequently.

28% of the region's average markup. A substantial number of gasoline stations make large changes in their pricing decisions over relatively short time periods.

We then relate our findings to five types of retail pricing models that appear relevant to explaining retail gasoline pricing. The first two types of models consist of static models. The pure strategy models (e.g., Thomadsen (2005)) predict that in each period retailers will charge the single-period profit-maximizing prices which vary with localized demand, competition, and marginal costs. An important implication of these models is they predict no inter-temporal price variation when costs and market structure remain constant. A second type of static model allows for mixed strategies in prices (e.g., Varian (1980)) that generate equilibria in which prices and margins vary even when costs and market structure remain constant. We then describe three types of dynamic models and formulate competition as a repeated (history-dependent) game and are thus also able to generate equilibriums in which prices and margins vary even when costs and market structure remain constant. There are three types of dynamic models: models of collusive behavior (e.g., Green and Porter (1984) and Haltiwanger and Harrington(1991)), models with history-dependent demand curves that lead to asymmetric price adjustment (e.g., Lewis (2005a)), and models of Edgeworth cycles (e.g., Maskin and Tirole (1988)).

While each of these models is consistent with some elements of the retail gasoline pricing we observe, none fit all the stylized facts. For example, while there is heterogeneity in gasoline station pricing (consistent with a model predicting constant margins), stations frequently change their margins (both absolutely and relatively). Static models predicting mixed strategies in prices fail to predict the persistence in pricing we observe. Our findings clearly show that a station's pricing is dynamic: pricing in week *t* depends on pricing week *t-1*. The existing dynamic models also do not comport well with our findings. While margins change dramatically during our sample period, there is no evidence of price wars. The shape of the retail margin distribution stays constant. Similarly, models of asymmetric price adjustment or Edgeworth cycles are also not supported by our data.

The remainder of paper is organized as follows. The next section provides a brief review of the empirical gasoline pricing literature, a summary of relevant institutional detail about gasoline retailing and describes our data. Section three presents our empirical findings. Section four discusses the various models of pricing behavior most likely to be applicable to retail gasoline. Section five relates these theoretical models to our empirical findings. Section six concludes and presents possible avenues for further work.

2.0   Literature Review, Background, and Data

Constrained by available data, researchers have historically examined either inter-temporal or inter-station price variation. The research on inter-temporal variation, often referred to as the "rockets and feathers" literature, uses pricing data at various levels of the industry (i.e., spot, rack and retail) usually aggregated over large geographic areas to examine the price response of gasoline at one level, e.g. retail, to a change in price at another level, e.g. wholesale. Some papers in this literature find that retail prices increase more quickly following increases to wholesale prices than decreases, (see, e.g., Borenstein et al (1997)), while others (e.g. Galeotti et al. (2003)) find the opposite result. The results of this literature are mixed and seem to depend on the time aggregation of the data (daily, weekly, or monthly), the level of the industry examined (refining, distribution, or retail), and the estimation technique. Although we find some statistical evidence of asymmetric adjustment, we find that this modeling approach leaves important features of the data unexplained.

The research on inter-station price variation uses station-level data either as a single-period cross-sectional or a short panel.[4] These papers have found that much of the inter-station variation retail price can be explained by brand affiliation, some measures of localized competition (typically a measure of localized station density and/or distance to the closest rival), and a handful of station attributes (e.g., if the station also performs repairs, has a convenience store, or offers full service gasoline). Our results suggest that these findings may not be robust across different time periods or geographic locales.

Our paper belongs to a relatively nascent (but rapidly growing) group of papers which lies at the convergence of these two branches of the empirical gasoline pricing literature and uses relatively long panels of weekly (or daily) station-level pricing data to examine the dynamics of station-level pricing behavior. Eckert and West (2003, 2004a, 2004b) and Noel (2005, 2007a, 2007b) analyze station-level dynamics, and find evidence of

---

[4] Examples of papers examining retail gasoline pricing in a cross section or short panel see, Slade (1992), Shepard (1990, 1991, 1993), Barron et al. (2000, 2004), and Hastings (2004).

Edgeworth cycles in station-level retail pricing. Lewis (2007) also finds evidence of Edgeworth cycles using a panel of aggregated (to the city) retail gasoline pricing. Lewis (2005a) verifies that the "rockets and feathers" pattern is present in station-level data in Southern California. Lewis (2005b) is the study most similar to ours. It examines retail price dispersion using a sample of station-level pricing data from southern California. In contrast to our paper, however, Lewis (2005b) focuses directly on relating price dispersion to models of consumer search while we focus on models of retailer pricing.

2.1 Institutional Detail

Gasoline stations are retailers. They receive gasoline from a distributor (sometimes vertically integrated) and resell it to consumers. Like other retailers, gasoline stations compete on prices, quality (location, cleanliness, speed of pumps), and bundles of services (convenience store, repair services). There are, however, a number of important characteristics of gasoline retailing that differentiate it from other types of retailing. First, the issue of consumers purchasing "bundles" of products is less important to gas stations than to other types of retailers, such as food or clothing. Virtually every consumer entering a gas station purchases gasoline, while only a subset will purchase other goods (beer, cigarettes, or repair services).[5] Because a low price on gasoline is attractive to *every* potential consumer, the price of gasoline is more strategic than the pricing of other products sold by the gas station.[6] Second, relative to many other products, gasoline is fairly homogeneous. These factors suggest consumer search for gasoline is easier than many other retail goods. Third, neither the station nor the consumer can hold meaningful inventories of the product. A tanker truck

---

[5] For example, convenience stores, which represent the largest retail channel of gasoline sales (approximately 75%) report that gasoline sales represent roughly 69.5% of convenience store revenues in 2003. National Association of Convenience Stores web page, visited 1/31/07.

[6] Lal and Matutes (1994) develop a model of retailers selling bundles of products with low prices on a subset of products to attract consumers. Hosken and Reiffen (2004) extend Lal and Matutes model showing that the low priced items are in most consumers' bundles.

holds 7,500 to 9,000 gallons of gasoline. A typically station sells more than 90,000 gallons a month which means over 10 deliveries a month.[7]

One advantage of studying gasoline retailing is that some measures of marginal cost, wholesale or "rack" prices for branded and unbranded gasoline, are observable to researchers.[8] The gas stations that purchase branded gas at the rack are owned and operated by individuals who, in essence, operate franchises. Other firms (sometimes the same firms selling branded gasoline, sometimes firms acting purely as distributors) will post unbranded prices for gasoline that will be sold at stations unaffiliated with a brand.

There are, however, two other channels of retail gasoline distribution for which marginal cost are unobserved. Stations that are owned and operated by a refiner (i.e., completely vertically integrated) "pay" an unobserved transfer price for gasoline. There are also a significant number of "lessee dealer" stations in Northern Virginia. These stations are owned by the refiner but operated by separate entities.[9] These stations pay an unobserved wholesale price for gasoline that is determined by the refiner. In addition, the wholesale price paid by different lessee dealers operating in the same metropolitan area may vary.[10] Thus, at any time, there may be a number of different marginal costs across stations within the same region. We follow the literature in viewing the posted rack prices as the opportunity cost of gasoline, since refiners and distributors choose to sell at that price.

We examine stations located in the Northern Virginia suburbs of Washington DC. This region likely contains all of the important retail gasoline competitors in Northern Virginia. While Northern Virginia is in the same metropolitan area as both Washington DC and Suburban Maryland, commuting patterns and the relative prices of gasoline in these

---

[7] For a discussion of the average level of gasoline sales by station and tanker delivery see, Federal Trade Commission, 2004, pp. 218 and 241.

[8] The wholesale distribution point of gasoline is refereed to as the "rack", the point where trucks obtain the gasoline for the retail stations. The terms rack and terminal are used synonymously.

[9] In Virginia refiners can not build new company owned and operated gasoline stations but the 1979 divorcement law allowed refiners to continue to operate the stations they owned.

[10] See Meyer and Fischer (2004) for an extensive description of lessee dealer pricing and zone pricing.

areas likely negates the impact of pricing in Maryland and DC on stations in Virginia. The regions in Virginia beyond our sample area likely do not contain many important competitors because there are very few stations in these regions with very little population.

2.2 Data

Our data come from three sources. We have a three year panel of average weekly retail prices for 272 stations in Northern Virginia. These data come from the Oil Price Information Service ("OPIS"), and are generated from fleet card[11] transaction data. We also have data from OPIS on the wholesale prices of both branded and unbranded gasoline at the closest rack to our stations, Fairfax, Virginia.

We have a census of all of the roughly 600 stations in Northern Virginia for 1997, 1998, and 1999 from New Image Marketing. The census consists of annual surveys of stations' addresses, attributes (e.g., whether the station has service bays, a convenience store, and the number of pumps), and a description of the station's vertical relationship with its supplier. While we do not observe the pricing of all stations, we are able to construct variables measuring the competitive environment each of the stations in our sample faces. Specifically, we calculate measures of station density (the number of stations located within different mileage bands of our sampled station) and the distance to the closest station.

Finally, we obtained information on neighborhood characteristics (measured at the zip-code level) from the U.S. Census. These variables, which include median household income, population, population density, and commuting time, are from the 2000 census and correspond to conditions in 1999.

---

[11] Fleet cards are often used by firms whose employees drive a lot for business purposes, e.g., salesman or insurance claims adjusters. Fleet cards are used to monitor what items employees charge to the firm. A station reports a price in a given week if one the fleet cards that OPIS observes was used at that station during the week. Most, but not all, stations in the sample are observed every week. Hence, the panel is unbalanced. We have dropped stations from the analysis that are observed very infrequently: a station is excluded if it is not observed for at least 10 weeks in a calendar year.

We examine three different measures of price. The retail price of gasoline is the price recorded at the pump (including taxes) for the most commonly sold variation of gasoline (87 octane). We use the average "branded rack" as our measure of wholesale price. This is defined as the average price of all of the "branded" gasoline's offered at the rack in a week. We have chosen the branded rack as our benchmark measure of wholesale price because the majority of stations sell a branded product. Our results, however, are robust to the choice of rack price.[12] Finally, we define a station's mark-up (margin) to be the retail price less the branded rack price and taxes. Thus, a station's margin corresponds to its incremental profit. Descriptive statistics for the data on OPIS sample of stations used in the pricing analysis as well as the descriptive statistics on the population of stations in Northern Virginia are presented in Table 1. On average there are almost 8.6 stations within 1.5 miles of the stations in both the OPIS sample the population. The other variables, station attributes and demographics, have similar means and standard deviations in both the OPIS sample and the population with two exceptions. First, the OPIS sample has a higher fraction of stations that sell only self service gasoline (84% vs. 74%). Second, the distribution of station management also differs between the two samples, e.g., 58% of stations in the OPIS sample are lessee dealers vs. 46% of stations in Northern Virginia.

The break down of station affiliations in our sample is presented in Table 2. The OPIS data set omits some major brands (specifically, Exxon and Amoco) as well as some minor brands and independents.[13] Due to the lack of Exxon and Amoco stations in our price data, there is proportional over sampling of the remaining brands such as Shell and Texaco.

---

[12] Branded rack prices are the wholesale prices for the refiner providing the gasoline, (such as Texaco, Exxon, or Mobil). Unbranded rack prices are the prices charged by a distributor (often, but not always a refiner) for gasoline that will ultimately be sold to consumers under the name of an independent gasoline retailer. During our sample the branded gasoline price is a few cents per gallon higher than unbranded gasoline price.

[13] Some brands (ordinarily) disallow OPIS from reporting their fleet card purchases, and some brands do not accept fleet cards (*e.g.*, ARCO). The decision to accept a fleet card is not made by each station but by brand.

3.0   Results

In this section we describe empirical findings about retail gasoline pricing. First, we find that the distribution of retail margins within a region shifts dramatically over time. While our data is consistent with a pattern of asymmetric price adjustment (price increases being passed through more quickly than price decreases), our findings suggest this explanation is incomplete. Second, we find that stations do not appear to follow simple pricing rules: both their margins and their prices relative to other stations fluctuate over time. While there is systematic heterogeneity in some stations' pricing, e.g., stations consistently charging relatively high or low prices, station characteristics (other than brand affiliation) and measures of localized competition are not good predictors of this heterogeneity. Third, we find that the systematic component of a station's pricing decision (the station's average relative price) changes, often substantially, from year to year.

3.1   Finding 1: Retail Margins Vary Substantially Over Time

Retail margins vary dramatically over time. Figure 1 shows the branded rack price of gasoline and the plot of the 25th, 50th, and 75th percentiles of the distribution of gasoline stations' retail margins (retail price less wholesale prices and taxes) by week from 1997 through 1999. During this time period the average retail margin was 14.4 cents per gallon, as high as 20.9 cents per gallon (in 1999), and as low as 5.7 cents (also in 1999). The figure also shows that the entire pricing distribution tends to shift over time; i.e., the spread between the 25th and 75th percentile is fairly stable, roughly 4 cents per gallon in 1997, and 5 cents in 1998 and 1999.

Although the margins in our dataset vary over time, they also exhibit a high degree of persistence. For example, the median margin is more than 17 cents per gallon for 26 consecutive weeks (averaging 19.4 cents) in 1997 and 1998 before falling to less than 14 cents per gallon (averaging 10.7 cents) for 12 weeks. Obviously, the change in retail profits associated with this change in margin is sizeable. While we do not observe output, it is reasonable to assume that changes in quantity are relatively small (gasoline demand is very inelastic), while the retail margin fell by 50%.[14]

3.2 Finding 2: Stations Do Not Follow Simple Pricing Rules

The wholesale price of gasoline is volatile. At the beginning of our sample the wholesale price of gasoline is approximately 75 cents per gallon. In early 1999 it fell to 35 cents before rising back to 75 cents per gallon in late 1999. The primary source of retail price variation in our data results from a gasoline station changing its price in response to a change in the wholesale price, or when the station changes its price relative to other stations. This can be seen most clearly by a simple decomposition of price; that is, decomposing overall price variation into between station and within station price variation. Figure 2 plots the percentage of within price variation for each year in our data set, and separately by station ownership type for each year. In 1997 and 1998 roughly 2/3 of retail price variation is generated by a station changing its prices over time, 1/3 of price variation is the result of differences in a station's mean pricing. In 1999 (when wholesale gasoline prices more than doubled) within price variation rose to 90%. There are some slight differences in the proportion of price variation by ownership type, however, the changes do not appear to be systematic. Company owned and operated stations, for example, have disproportionately low within price variation in 1997, but not in 1998 or 1999. A station's ownership type does not appear to be important source of either the within or between price variation in our data.

Because changes in wholesale costs are such an important component of retail price variation and are not the focus of our study, we define retail price variation as the deviations

---

[14] Our finding of dramatic changes in retail margins is potentially consistent with recent empirical research on asymmetric price adjustment in retail gasoline markets sometimes referred to as the "rockets and feathers" literature (see, e.g., Borenstein et al. (1997) and Lewis (2005a)). These studies find that increases in wholesale gasoline prices are passed through more quickly than wholesale price decreases. While there is some statistical evidence of asymmetric pass through of wholesale costs in our data, the coefficients of estimated asymmetric price adjustment model were not economically plausible and differed substantially from those found in the existing literature (see section 5.4).

about the region's mean price at a point in time. We analyze retail price dispersion by examining the residuals from the following regression:

$$(1) \quad p_{it} = \sum_t \gamma_t (Week\ Indicator_{it}) + e_{it}$$

where $p_{i,t}$ is station i's gasoline price in week t, and the γ_t are the coefficients corresponding to weekly indicators. We estimate equation (1) using data for each station and time period. The frequency distribution of the estimated error terms (e_{it}) is presented in Figure 3. Most prices are very close to the mean: 56% and 71% of prices are within 2.5 cents and 3.5 cents of the mean, respectively. The tails of the distribution are quite thick. Roughly 3.5% of prices are more than 10 cents from the mean. To illustrate further, we plot a normal frequency distribution with the same mean and standard deviation as the observed residuals (mean zero, standard deviation of 3.99 cents). If the residuals were normal, we would expect to see 47% and 62% of prices within 2.5 and 3.5 cents of the mean, and 1.2% of prices more than 10 cents from the mean. We can easily reject the null that the residuals have a normal distribution.[15]

The general pattern seen for the pooled data also holds when looking at the residuals separately by year.[16] While the shape of the distribution differs somewhat across years (prices appear less disperse in 1997 than either 1998 or 1999), most gasoline prices are very close to the mean: 75%, 69% and 66% are within 3.5 cents of the mean in 1997, 1998 and 1999. Further, the tails are thick: roughly 2% of prices are more than ten cents from the mean in 1997 and 4% of prices are more than ten cents from the mean in 1998 and 1999.[17] An implication of this result is that models estimated using maximum likelihood and an

_____

[15] The kurtosis of the residual distribution is 6.07, the p-value for the test of normality is essentially zero. A normal random variable has a kurtosis of 3, variables with a kurtosis greater than 3 are said to be leptokurtic.

[16] See Appendix Figures 1-3.

[17] If the residuals were normally distributed, the expected proportion of prices within 3.5 cents of the mean would be: 68%, 60% and 59% and the proportion of prices more than 10 cents from the mean would be 0.5%, 1.6%, and 1.9% in 1997, 1998 and 1999. The residual distributions in 1997, 1998, and 1999 have kurtosis of 9.21, 5.45, and 4.55. In each year, we reject the null of normality of the residual distribution with a p-value of zero.

assumption that errors are normally distributed may yield inefficient parameter estimates, see, e.g., White (1982).

While retail gasoline prices are tightly distributed about the mean, some stations charge prices very different than the mean. Further, average retail markups change substantially during the sample period (by 50%), and these different regimes are persistent. Despite significant changes in retail margins and gasoline prices over time, the shape of the distribution of prices about the median margin does not change very much – during our sample period the inter-quartile range is typically between 3 and 6 cents. This leads to a question: is the gasoline pricing distribution stable over time? Do individual stations pick a price relative to their rivals and maintain that price, or do stations change their relative position in the pricing distribution?

We find that gasoline stations change their *relative* prices frequently. While some stations charge systematically higher or lower prices, relative prices change frequently. Finally, in contrast to many previous papers, station characteristics, other than brand affiliation, do not explain much of a station's average relative pricing.

We analyze a firm's price changes by defining the firm's relative price in week t to be the residual from equation (1); i.e., the difference between station i's price in week t and the mean price of all stations in our sample in week t. We round the residual to the nearest cent and construct a Markov transition matrix where the elements of the matrix show the probability of being y cents above (below) the mean in period t conditional on being x cents above (below) the mean in period $t-1$. The matrix is presented in Appendix Table 1, however, a more intuitive understanding of the matrix can be seen from graphing the conditional probability distributions in Figure 4.[18] For example, Figure 4.J plots the probability distribution of a gasoline station's price in period t conditional on the station charging the region's mean price in period $t-1$; i.e., the residual from equation (1) in period t-

---

[18] To facilitate presentation we have omitted large deviations from the region's mean price in constructing Figure 4 and appendix Table 1. We plot the Markov transition matrices if the previous period's relative price (the residual from eq. (1)) is between -9 and 9. This limits the number of frequency distributions presented in Figure 4 to 19. Similarly, we also truncated the distribution of the current period's relative price to be between -15 and 15. Together, these restrictions omit roughly 10% of the pricing observations from the figure.

1 rounds to zero. Figure 4.J shows that the probability that a station will continue to charge the mean price in the region in period *t* is 0.47, and the probability the station will be charging a price within a penny of the region's mean in period *t* is 0.84.

There are two key observations from Figure 4. First, there is persistence in gasoline stations' relative prices. The modal choice of a station is to maintain its relative pricing from week to week; i.e., if a station is 4 cents below the mean in period *t-1*, it is most likely to be 4 cents below the mean in period *t*. Second, despite this persistence, for all of the conditional probability distributions, the mode is less than 50%. Thus, more than 50% of the time a station's relative price will change by at least one cent each week. The shape of the probability distributions of stations charging low prices in period *t* looks very different than stations charging high prices in period *t*. Stations charging relatively low prices have more mass at or near the mode than those stations charging relatively high prices (compare Figures 4.A-4.D to 4.O-4.S). This suggests that stations charging high prices converge to the mean more quickly than stations charging low prices. The transition matrices show that while gas stations periodically charge high prices, they do not maintain abnormally high prices for very long. Low prices, however, appear to be more persistent.

To examine the importance of this heterogeneity in characterizing retail gasoline pricing, we control for both time effects and time invariant-station effects in equation (2) below,

$$(2) \quad p_{it} = \sum_i \theta_i (Station\ Indicator_{it}) + \sum_t \gamma_t (Week\ Indicator_{it}) + u_{it}$$

where the θ_i are gasoline station specific fixed-effects; that is, θ_i is station *i*'s mean relative price where $\theta_i = 0$ corresponds to the station whose average relative price is the mean price. Equation (2) models stations pursuing a static pricing strategy with the markup a function of (time-invariant) observed and unobserved attributes (as measured by the θ_i's). The interpretation of the residuals from equation (2) is very different than equation (1). For example, u_{it} is now the deviation from station *i*'s pricing in period *t* after controlling for station *i*'s time-invariant effects. If we observe persistence in a station's residual, u_{it}, then it means that the station is systematically charging higher or lower prices *than its typical relative price*. Not surprisingly, equation (2) explains more of the variation in retail pricing than (1). The R-squared increases from 0.88 to 0.95 and we are able to explain most of the large deviations in stations' prices. Figure 5 plots the residuals from regression 2 and shows that

14

only 0.9% of residuals are more than 10 cents from the mean (compared to 3.4% from the regression in equation (1)).

Figure 6, constructed analogously to Figure 4, presents the Markov transition matrix with the residuals from equation (2).[19] The interpretation of Figure 6, however, differs from Figure 4, because it shows the probabilities of transitions between consecutive weeks where prices are measured relative to a specific *station's* average relative price (rather than relative to the average price in Northern Virginia). For example, in Figure 6.O, we see a station charging a price 5 cents more than its mean price in week *t-1* is predicted to be charging a price 5 cents more than its mean in week *t* with probability 0.31. There are two notable differences between Figures 4 and 6. First, controlling for a station's mean relative pricing (θ_i) explains a great deal of the persistence in pricing. This can most clearly be seen by the decrease in the modal prices in moving from Figure 4 to Figure 6 when a station is not charging a price close to its mean price; that is, excluding Figures 6.I, 6.J, and 6.K. While the modal price charged in week *t* is the price charged in *t-1* in both figures, this mode is lower in Figure 6 than Figure 4. Second, there is quicker convergence to the mean in Figure 6. A station charging a price above its *own* mean is predicted to return to its *own* mean price more quickly than a station charging a higher price than the *region's* mean is predicted to return to the *region's* mean price. It is interesting to note, however, that even controlling for a station's average pricing, the predicted pricing distribution at time *t* depends on *t-1*; that is, pricing decisions are inherently dynamic.

While this analysis is informative, it has compared prices over a large region and so potentially misses some important aspects of localized competition. In densely populated Northern Virginia, it is unlikely that a gas station considers the prices of stations 10 miles away when setting its prices. It is easy to imagine that stations develop simple pricing rules, such as maintaining the second lowest price among the ten closest stations, or being 3 cents lower than a store with a prime location.

_____

[19] Appendix Table 2 contains the matrix corresponding to Figure 6. As in constructing Figure 4, we have omitted observations if the previous period's relative price is between -9 and 9, and if the current period's relative price to be between -15 and 15. Together, these restrictions omit roughly 8% of the pricing observations from Figure 6.

We examine localized pricing by determining each station's price position relative to its 9 closest rivals each week (where a rank of 1 corresponds to the lowest price and 10 to the highest).[20] To illustrate a station's rank over time, we plotted the weekly price ranks of a Crown station and a Mobil station in our data set (see Figure 7). The relative pricing patterns for the two stations are noticeably different. The Crown station charges very low relative prices each period, and is most often the lowest. This pattern is not unique to this Crown station: all Crown stations in our sample persistently charge relatively low prices. In contrast, the Mobil station changes its relative position in the pricing distribution frequently, sometimes being the highest and sometimes the lowest priced station. While this particular Mobil station is an outlier in changing its relative price very frequently, similar patterns are seen for many other stations in our data.

Because it is not feasible to report the relative rank series for every station, we create an analogous aggregate measure. We construct a Markov transition matrix and graphically present it in Figure 8. This figure has the same interpretation as Figures 4 and 6. Figure 8 shows a very similar pattern to the week to week price changes of the relative prices from all of Northern Virginia. The modal strategy for a station is to maintain its relative pricing position from week to week. Stations charging prices close to the median of the distribution (a rank of 4, 5, 6, or 7) are much more likely to change relative position from week to week than stations at the high and low end of the distribution. The same pattern emerges when viewing stations prices relative to a narrower group of stations consisting of its four closest rivals (see Figure 9). Stations charging low or high prices in one week (rank 1 or 5) are more likely to charge low/high prices in the subsequent week than stations prices near the median (ranks 2, 3, and 4).

---

[20] Our price data is a sample of stations. We analyze station prices relative to the 9 closest stations *in our sample*. This set of stations differs from the 9 closest in the population. While this distinction could be important, we think it is not. As is discussed below, the pattern in relative ranks is very similar to the pattern in relative prices seen in Figures 4 and 6.

3.2.1   Estimating a Station's Idiosyncratic Pricing Function

Many prior studies which examine localized gasoline pricing have been limited to either cross-sectional or a short panel of data.[21] These data limitations have forced researchers both to use observable characteristics rather than station fixed effects, and to assume that the relationship between stations' prices and their measurable characteristics are relatively constant over time.[22] The richness of our dataset allows us to evaluate the robustness of these assumptions. In general, we find that observable station characteristics (other than a station's brand affiliation) are poor predictors of station-specific pricing.

We begin by estimating a specification including the key control variables from the literature. Specifically we estimate a station's retail margin in each week (markup over the wholesale price of branded gas) as a function of station attributes,[23] demographics corresponding to the station's zip code,[24] indicators for the brand of gasoline sold, localized competition, and the vertical relationship between the station and its gasoline supplier as in equation (3) below where i is the store index and t is the week index.[25]

$$(3)\quad M\arg in_{it} = \alpha_k + \sum_l \gamma_l (Localized\ Competition\ Variables_{it}) +$$
$$\sum_m \delta_m (Demographics_{it}) + \sum_n \beta_n (Station\ Characteristics_{it}) +$$
$$\sum_o \pi_o (Vertical\ Relationship_{it}) + \sum_p \theta_p (Brand\ Indicator_{it}) + \sum_q \lambda_q (Year_{it}) + \mu_{it}$$

---

[21] Eckert and West (2004a, 2004b), Lewis (2005a, 2005b) and Noel (2007a) are exceptions.

[22] The goal of these studies is not to measure the returns to different station characteristics or brand. In most cases, the authors are trying to control for other factors that affect gasoline prices and include these characteristics as control variables. In some of the short panel studies, (such as, Hastings (2004)), authors use station level fixed effects as controls.

[23] A subset of station characteristics were missing for 8 of the stations in our data set. For this reason, regression (3) was estimated using data for the 264 rather than 272 stations.

[24] Because gasoline stations likely draw customers from a region larger than a census block, we use zip code level measures of the demographic variables.

[25] Because individual stations appear many times in the data set, we estimate clustered standard errors (at the station level).

We construct two types of variables to measure localized competition similar to those used in the literature. The first set of variables measure the density of localized competition: the number of stations located with 1.5 miles of station i and the distance between station i and the next closest station.[26] Presumably, other things equal, a greater density of localized competition should result in lower retail margins. The next set of variables measures the *type* of nearby competitors. Hastings (2004), for example, finds that a given gas station charges lower prices when facing an unbranded competitor, and higher prices when facing only branded competitors. In our sample, there are four station brands that charge systematically low gasoline prices: Coastal, Crown, RaceTrac, and Sheetz. Each of these stations can be viewed as unbranded in the sense defined by Hastings (2004).[27] We define a variable that measures the proportion of the ten closest stations that are one of these four brands. We construct an analogous variable to measure which stations face disproportionately high priced competitors: the fraction of the ten closest competitors that are Exxon or Mobil stations (the two market leaders). If vertically integrated gasoline stations charge different retail prices than other stations, then a gas station competing with many vertically integrated gasoline stations may charge different prices than a firm competing with independent stations. To allow for this possibility, we construct two variables that measure the level of vertical integration of nearby stations. The fraction of the ten closest stations that are either 1) owned an operated by a refiner, or 2) are owned by a refiner but leased to an operator.

The results from estimating this equation are shown in the first column of Table 3. Consistent with the literature, we find that brand effects are very important predictors of retail margins. Company owned and operated stations also earn higher margins, roughly 1.5 cents. This finding does not, however, imply that vertically integration causes retailers to charge higher prices. Because of Virginia's divorcement law, refiners can only own and operate stations that were in operation before 1979. In northern Virginia, older stations are,

---

[26] These measures of localized competition are identical to those used in Barron et al. (2004).

[27] While Crown stations were technically branded (owned and operated by a small refiner), Crown operated its stations like an unbranded retailer. That is, Crown did not engage in extensive advertising to develop a gasoline brand like the major U.S. gasoline refiners, e.g., Exxon, Mobil, or Shell.

on average, located in more densely populated areas with higher land costs. Thus, this increased margin may result because older stations are located in more valuable locations.

Interestingly, we find that although the station's demographic environment (median household income, population, population density, and median commuting time) are important predictors of margins, none of the stations' physical attributes (e.g., having a convenience store) appear to be important predictors. The estimated coefficients on the stations' physical attributes are both statistically and economically (all less than a penny) insignificant.

The remaining columns of Table 3 report the estimates when we allow the coefficients to vary across years. A few findings are worth noting. First, the estimated coefficients on the demographic variables change significantly across years. Whether this is the result of measurement error (these variables come from the 2000 census and correspond to conditions in 1999), or a change in the pricing function is unclear. Second, the estimated brand coefficients for those stations which make up a large share of our sample, Mobil, Crown, Shell and Texaco, vary from year to year. Third, two of the estimated localized competition variables are somewhat significant, however only in one year. In the 1997 regression, an increase in the fraction of nearby low priced stations is predicted to lower retail margins, as is a decrease in the distance to the next closest station. However, the size of the economic effect in both cases is small. The maximum value of the low priced competition variable is .3, implying that retail margins drop by 1.2 cents relative to facing *no* low priced competition. Similarly, decreasing the distance to the closest gas station by on standard deviation (.34 miles) is predicted to lower prices by about 0.33 cents.

In sum, we do not find an important consistent relationship between a station's margin and either station characteristics or localized competition. This finding is likely not an artifact of the specific functional form used to measure competition or station characteristics. Alternative measures of localized competition; e.g., including the number of stores within 1/2 mile, 1 mile, 3 miles, and interactions of these measures, are not consistent predictors of retail margins (results available on request). Similarly, we have examined many other station attributes (including measures of nearby traffic conditions) and do not find a relationship between these attributes and retail gasoline markups.[28]

As noted above, Crown stations followed a different pricing strategy during our sample period than other stations in Northern Virginia.[29] In particular, Crown stations charge relatively low prices independent of the localized competitive environment. For this reason, we fully interact a Crown indicator variable with all of the other variables in the pricing equation – effectively dropping the Crown stations from the sample. The results for the non-Crown coefficients appear in Table 4.

The key difference we see in estimating the model for the non-Crown stations is the importance of one of the variables measuring the density of local competition is statistically significant in the pooled model and in the models estimated separately for 1997 and 1998. However, the estimated effect is still fairly small. Having the closest station one standard deviation closer (0.34 miles) is predicted to lower prices about 0.5 cents. While this finding causes our results to look more similar to the literature, it also suggests that the pricing function implied by equation (3) is not uniform across stations.

3.3   Finding 3: Many Stations Change Their Pricing Strategy Over Time

The pricing pattern we see in Figure 6, after controlling for both time and station fixed-effects, suggests that stations change relative prices over time. To examine this we estimate a slightly modified version of equation (2) where we allow the station effects to vary by calendar year (q=1997, 1998, 1999):

---

[28]While the change in retail gasoline markups over time could theoretically be the result of collusive behavior among gasoline wholesalers supplying Northern Virginia, recent evidence suggests this is not the explanation. Taylor and Hosken (2007) examined the wholesale (rack) price of gasoline at Fairfax, the supply point for Northern Virginia and found that the average wholesale price in Fairfax during this time period reflected the product price in the Gulf, the source of marginal supply, and the cost of transport.

[29] All but one of the Crown gasoline stations in our sample are owned and operated by the refiner. These stations are vertically integrated and the refiner controls retail pricing.

20

$$(4) \quad p_{it} = \sum_t \gamma_t (\text{Week Indicators}_{it}) + \sum_{i,q} \theta_i^q (\text{Station Indicators}_{it})(\text{Year}_{it}) + w_{it}$$

If a station's idiosyncratic relative pricing changes from year to year $\left(\theta_i^{1997} \neq \theta_i^{1998} \neq \theta_i^{1999} \right)$, we conclude the station is pursuing a different pricing strategy. We use two different approaches to measure a station's pricing changes year to year.

First, we record the percentile corresponding to a station's estimated fixed-effect in the store effect distribution in year k; i.e., we rank all θ_i^q from smallest to largest and record the percentile corresponding to each θ_i^q. We then calculate the difference in a station's percentile between each pair of years in our data set (1997 vs. 1998, 1998 vs. 1999, and 1997 vs. 1999).[30] These results are shown in the first section of Table 5. The table shows that small changes in a station's relative pricing are fairly common. For example, between 1997 and 1998 more than half of gasoline stations change their relative position in the pricing distribution by at least 10 percentile points. Further, some stations dramatically change their position in the pricing distribution, e.g., between 1997 and 1998 4% of gasoline stations estimated store-effects changed by more than 50 percentile points in the pricing distribution.

Second, we measure the absolute change (in cents) in the station effects from year to year. In Table 5, we see that many of the changes in station effects are statistically significant. In comparing stores observed in 1997 and 1998, 1998 and 1999, and 1997 and 1999, we find that 33%, 27%, and 45% (respectively) of changes in estimated store effects are statistically significant with a (conditional) mean change in price of between 3 and 4 cents per period. The observed changes in pricing strategy are economically important. For example, in our data, the mean margin is roughly 14 cents per gallon.

4.0   Existing Models of Retail Pricing

Because of the richness of these data, the results described in Section III can shed light on the ability of various retail pricing models to explain behavior. In this regard, we

---

[30] In estimating equation 4 we require at least 10 observations per year. With this restriction we had 170, 163, and 193 comparisons between 1997 and 1998, 1997 and 1999, and 1998 and 1999 respectively.

suffer from an embarrassment of riches -- many pricing models appear relevant to retail gasoline. Because there are so many, we use this section to first relate these models and their empirical predictions to one another. The next section relates those predictions to our findings.

We are aware of five different types of models of pricing behavior that may be applied to retail gasoline. The first two types of models assume that each retailer's actions in each period are independent of prior play. The first set limits stations to play pure strategies. These models predict that in each period retailers will charge the single-period profit-maximizing prices which will vary with localized demand, competition, and marginal costs. An important implication is these models predict no inter-temporal price variation when costs and market structure remain constant. Manuszak (2002) and Thomadsen (2005) are typical examples of this modeling approach. Although his model's complexity prohibits one from making definitive statements about its predictions for margins, in practice, Manuszak finds that his model generates roughly constant markups over time when demand follows a mixed logit.[31]

The second type of model allows for mixed strategies, and thus generates equilibria in which prices and margins vary even when costs and market structure remain constant. Varian (1980) provides an explanation of why a retailer would vary retail prices, independent of changes in wholesale prices that appears appropriate for gasoline retailing.[32] In Varian's

---

[31] See, for example, Manuszak's (2002) Figure 4.

[32] There are models of retailing which generate retail price changes independent of costs, but the features that drive these price changes are not present in retail gasoline. Conlisk et al. (1984), Sobel (1984) and Pesendorfer (2002) examine how changes in retail prices can be used as a means of price discrimination. These models include purchases that can be shifted over time (consumers either wait to purchase or carrying inventory). Pashigian (1988) and Pashigian and Bowen (1991) develop models for goods with a "fashion" element where prices systematically decline over a fashion season independent of wholesale costs. Hoch et al. (1994) examines how every day low priced firms and high-low price firms can both exist in the same market at the same time. Hoch et al. examines retailers selling a bundle of goods to consumers (such as food retailers) where the retailers offer differential markups on products in the bundle. As discussed earlier, this modeling approach is less appropriate for

model, consumers are heterogeneous in their willingness to search for low prices; some buy only at the first retailer they encounter, others compare prices and buy from the retailer offering the lowest price. Consequently, each retailer faces a tradeoff between charging a high price and selling only to consumers who do not search, versus charging a low price and potentially also selling to consumers who do search. Varian shows that the only symmetric equilibrium features mixed strategies, where all retailers choose their price from a continuous distribution with no mass points. In this equilibrium each retailer changes his price each period. Baye et al. (1992) show that asymmetric equilibria also exist when using Varian's modeling approach. Specifically, a subset of retailers can always charge a high price (equal to a consumer's willingness to pay) and only sell to customers who do not search, while the remainder of retailers play a mixed strategy identical to the strategy examined by Varian.[33]

Other models formulate competition as a repeated (history-dependent) game and are thus generate equilibria in which prices and margins vary even when costs and market structure remain constant. These dynamic models can be grouped into three categories: models of collusive behavior, models with history-dependent demand curves that lead to asymmetric price adjustment, and models of Edgeworth cycles.

A number of papers use collusive equilibria with price wars to explain changes in margins over time. Green and Porter (1984) provide a model of collusive behavior that relies on imperfect monitoring to generate periodic price wars in equilibrium. Although they explicitly model competition in industries characterized by quantity competition, commonly known cost functions, and imperfect monitoring, their model can be extended to cover industries with price competition where the uncertainty is over the cost functions rather than the price. For example, Athey and Bagwell (2001) and Athey et al. (2004) model an infinitely repeated Bertrand game with publicly observed prices and private i.i.d. cost shocks, which closely matches many of the features of retail gasoline competition. Applying a semi-parametric approach to examine stations' pricing behavior directly, Slade (1987, 1992) finds

---

gasoline stations which are more like single product retailers.

[33] Hong et al. (2002) examines a dynamic version of Varian's model where the consumers who search can also store the good for future consumption. Because gasoline cannot effectively be stored for future consumption by consumers (in contrast to grocery products), this model is not relevant for retail gasoline pricing.

evidence of a price war in Vancouver, Canada in 1983. She finds that stations' pricing behavior – in particular, stations' responses to their competitors' prices – varies over time.

Rotemberg and Saloner (1986) also offer a model of collusion that predicts fluctuating margins. In their model collusion breaks down during periods of relatively high demand, due to the fact that during those periods the gains from cheating are more likely to outweigh the subsequent punishments during lower demand periods. In an extension of this model, Haltiwanger and Harrington (1991) show that an increase in expected costs should lower the likelihood of collusion in the current period. Borenstein and Shepard (1996) test this theory using data on retail gasoline margins. Using a panel of city level data, they find that current retail margins increase in response to higher anticipated demand and fall in response to an anticipated increase in wholesale prices.

A second group of dynamic models stem from the recent empirical gasoline pricing literature focused on the asymmetric adjustment of the retail price of gasoline to changes in wholesale price. Lewis (2005a) provides theoretical underpinnings for these findings by formulating a "reference price" model that leads consumers to search less when prices are falling. In his model, consumers are slow to update their expectations about the distribution of prices and search less when prices are falling. This generates a kinked residual demand curve which in turn leads to asymmetric effects of marginal cost shocks on retail prices.

A third group of dynamic models stem from a model proposed by Maskin and Tirole (1988). In these models, stations play an alternating-move game choosing prices from a discrete grid. In equilibrium, stations undercut one another on price until it becomes unprofitable, at which point stations begin a new cycle by charging a high price. Although the original theoretical model relies on a number of assumptions inconsistent with retail gasoline competition, Noel (2005) has shown that cycling equilibria are still possible under considerably weaker conditions. Eckert (2002, 2003) and Eckert and West (2003, 2004a, 2004b) find evidence consistent with Edgeworth cycles in several Canadian cities, as does Noel (2007a, 2007b). One shortcoming of these models is that it can be difficult to determine when and whether stations are in a cycling equilibrium. Eckert (2002) and Noel (2005) use a Markov switching regression to determine this.

5.0 Evaluating theories of retail pricing for gasoline markets

The models described in the previous section have general predictions about the distribution of retail prices. In this section of the paper we describe how well each model matches our empirical findings. While no one theory can be expected to fully characterize the market place, we find substantial shortcomings in each approach.

5.1 Static Games with Pure Strategies

Modeling gasoline stations as charging a fixed markup over cost; i.e., modeling a station's decision using pure strategies as in Manuszak (2002) and Thomadsen (2005), has some empirical support. Our findings suggest that a large fraction of the retail gasoline price variation can be explained by including time effects, which control for common wholesale price changes, and station effects, which non-parametrically control for station specific localized demand, competition, and costs. In particular, the use of time-invariant store effects explains most of the large differences between a station's price and the market price. This can be seen by comparing the residual plots from Figures 3 (which only controls for time effects) and Figure 5 (which also controls for station effects). The evidence strongly suggests that gasoline stations have systematically different mean prices.

We see two important inconsistencies between these models and our findings. First, prices change substantially from period to period, suggesting that a fixed markup model is potentially missing important aspects of a gasoline station's pricing behavior. This can most clearly be seen by examining the plot of the Markov Transition Matrix in Figure 6. This figure shows us that even controlling for the systematic component of a station's pricing, there is still a substantial probability that the station will be charging a different relative price in subsequent periods. Further, the matrix shows that the movement back to mean pricing takes many periods. For example, if a station is charging a price at least 5 cents less than its mean price (an event that occurs about 3% of the time) the probability it will charge a price within a penny of its mean price in the next period is less than 10%. Clearly, there are dynamic components to pricing. Second, while there is a systematic aspect of a station's pricing, a significant fraction of stations appear to change where they are in the pricing distribution from year to year. The fraction changing relative price is large, nearly 30%, and the changes in a station's position in the price distribution can be substantial. Together these two inconsistencies reject a static modeling approach that predicts that gasoline stations have either constant margins or maintain a constant relative position in the pricing distribution.

Finally, even though there are systematic differences in mean price across stations, implementation of the modeling approach may be difficult because of data limitations. In our data, only a station's brand affiliation and measures of localized demand (zip-code level demographics) explain a sizeable fraction of a station's systematic mark up. The failure of either station amenities or measures of localized competition to explain station markups is disappointing. To credibly identify these types of models, the econometrician must observe characteristics of stations that both vary across stations and are associated with price. Equally troubling is that some brands behave very differently than others for unknown reasons. Crown gas stations were low price leaders in the Northern Virginia suburbs. As Figure 7 demonstrates, Crown systematically was the lowest priced gas station. To our knowledge there is no set of variables that would allow us to *a priori* predict this behavior.

5.2   Static Games with Mixed Strategies

Some aspects of gasoline pricing are consistent with prices being generated by mixed strategy similar to Varian (1980). We find that the modal choice for a gasoline station is to change its price each week. This is consistent with Varian's model, which has no mass-points. Strictly speaking, all firms in Varian's model should have the same mean price (retailers in Varian's model are identical and thus draw prices from the same distribution). However, it would not be difficult to extend the model to incorporate firm heterogeneity into the model (e.g., allow station's to face either different numbers of competitors or different fractions of consumers who search) which would generate different pricing distributions for different gas stations.

The more important inconsistency between Varian's model and our results is that while prices change every period, the model implies that each price draw should come from the same pricing distribution. Empirically, this implication is clearly violated. Figure 6, for example, shows that the price distribution for time *t+1* depends importantly on the price at time *t*. The modal price at time *t+1* is the price at time *t*, and the pricing distribution at time *t+1* is tightly centered around the price at time *t*. While this result could be explained by assuming that gasoline stations experience idiosyncratic autoregressive cost shocks, we find this explanation unlikely. Instead, it appears that a model of true dynamics; in which recent history matters, is required to explain changes in a gasoline's relative margin over time.

There is evidence that some retailers play very different pricing strategies; that is, some firms may play a mixed-price strategy while other firms maintain a relative position in the pricing distribution. However, in contrast to the prediction in Baye et al. (1992), the stations that maintain their position in the pricing distribution charge a systematically *low* rather than a *high* price. Thus asymmetric equilibria generated by Varian's modeling approach do not explain the asymmetric pricing behavior seen in our sample of retail gasoline stations.

5.3   Repeated Games with Collusion

A prediction of tacit collusion models (especially Green and Porter) is that average margins should vary over time (price wars). In an environment in which sellers are differentiated, this would translate into shifts in the price distribution, in which the shape of the distribution remains more or less constant, but the mean changes. As noted the price distribution does have this property. If the characteristics of firms do not change, this model would imply that a firm's price (relative to the mean) would remain fixed in all collusive periods. We find, however, that in every time period, including periods of high and low margins, firms change their relative position in the pricing distribution.[34] That is, the mechanism that supports collusion in these models is that decreases in prices by one firm are met by subsequent decreases in price for all firms. Hence, if a significant fraction of firms are changing their relative price every period, the model would suggest that the market would always be in the penalty phase.

While our finding that gasoline stations frequently change their position in the pricing distribution suggests collusion is unlikely, Borenstein and Sheppard (1996) (B&S) found empirical evidence consistent with model of collusion developed by Rotemberg and

---

[34] We have recalculated the transition matrix shown in Figure 6 separately by year and find the same pattern. Gasoline stations are more likely than not to change their prices every period in each year.

Saloner (1986) and extended by Haltiwanger and Harrington (1991). We conduct a test similar to B&S to determine if the pattern they found in retail margins exists in our data. The logic underlying B&S's test is that retailers anticipate future wholesale gasoline prices because there is a lag in the pass thru of crude price changes to wholesale price changes. An anticipated increase in wholesale costs is predicted to lower future retailer profits which leads to cheating on the collusive agreement in the current period. In other words, an anticipated increase in costs should lower the likelihood of retail collusion today. Thus, we should expect (and B&S found) that an increase in expected rack prices will lower current period margins.

B&S used a panel of prices (measured at the city level) from 43 cities over 72 months for their test. In conducting our test, we use the aggregate rack and retail prices from our sample. The first step is to forecast wholesale prices. Then we estimated a retail markup equation that was a function of anticipated wholesale price. We follow B&S's modeling approach as closely as possible. However, there are two important differences in our approach due to differences in our data sets. First, our study examines weekly data rather than monthly data. For this reason, our coefficient estimates are not directly comparable to B&S. Second, we do not have access to quantity data for Northern Virginia. Thus, our estimated margin equations do not include current or anticipated future demand as in B&S.[35]

Future rack prices are estimated to be a function of the lagged rack and crude price, and two lags of the change in crude and rack prices. In addition, the forecasting equation allows for asymmetric price adjustment; that is increases in lagged crude or rack prices can have different effects on expected rack prices than decreases. The forecasting equation, (4) below, also includes an error correction term; i.e., the lags of the rack and crude price.

$$(4) \quad RACK_t = a_0 + a_1 \Delta RACK_{t-1}^+ + a_2 \Delta RACK_{t-2}^+ + a_3 \Delta RACK_{t-1}^- + a_4 \Delta RACK_{t-2}^-$$
$$+ a_5 \Delta CRUDE_{t-1}^+ + a_6 \Delta CRUDE_{t-2}^+ + a_7 \Delta CRUDE_{t-1}^- + a_8 \Delta CRUDE_{t-2}^-$$
$$+ a_9 RACK_{t-1} + a_{10} CRUDE_{t-1} + \sum_{j=1}^{11} D_j^4 M_{jt} + e_t^4$$

$RACK_t$ is the average wholesale price for branded gasoline at the Fairfax rack in week t, $CRUDE_t$ is the spot price (per gallon) of West Texas Intermediate crude oil at Cushing, OK in week t (the most commonly quoted U.S. crude price), $\Delta RACK_t = RACK_t - RACK_{t-1}$,

---

[35] The equations we estimate closely parallel B&S's equations 1, 2, and 4 (See pages 439-441).

$$\Delta CRUDE_t = CRUDE_t - CRUDE_{t-1}, \quad \Delta RACK_t^+ = \Delta RACK_t \text{ if } \Delta RACK_t > 0, \text{ otherwise}$$

$$\Delta RACK_t^+ = 0, \quad \Delta RACK_t^- = \Delta RACK_t \text{ if } \Delta RACK_t < 0, \quad \Delta RACK_t > 0, \text{ otherwise}$$

$$\Delta RACK_t^- = 0, \quad \Delta CRUDE_t^+ \text{ and } \Delta CRUDE_t^- \text{ are defined similarly, the } M_{jt} \text{ are month}$$

indicators (included to control for seasonality), and the coefficients corresponding to the month indicators and the disturbance have a superscript that corresponds to the equation number.

Given the expected future rack price, we then estimate two versions of the margin equation which closely parallel those in B&S. The first, equation (5) below, specifies a simple lag structure.

$$(5) \quad MARGIN_t = b_0 + b_1 RACK_t + b_2 EXPECTED\ RACK_{t+1} + b_3 \Delta RACK_t + \sum_{j=1}^{11} D_j^5 M_{jt} + e_t^5$$

$MARGIN_t = RET_t - RACK_t$, RET_t is the average retail price in our sample in week t, and $EXPECTED\ RACK_{t+1}$ is the expected rack price in week $t+1$ which is estimated by equation (4) above. The second margin equation, (6) below, uses a more general lag structure that allows the current margin to be a function of multiple lags and includes an error correction term. In addition, like equation (4), this specification allows for asymmetric adjustment.

$$(6) \quad MARGIN_t = c_0 + c_1 EXPECTED\ RACK_{t+1} + c_2 RACK_{t-1} + c_3 RET_{t-1} + c_4 \Delta RACK_t^+$$
$$+ c_5 \Delta RACK_{t-1}^+ + c_6 \Delta RACK_{t-2}^+ + c_7 \Delta RACK_t^- + c_8 \Delta RACK_{t-1}^- + c_9 \Delta RACK_{t-2}^-$$
$$+ c_8 \Delta RET_{t-1}^+ + c_9 \Delta RET_{t-2}^+ + c_{10} \Delta RET_{t-1}^- + c_{11} \Delta RET_{t-2}^-$$
$$+ \sum_{j=1}^{11} D_j^6 M_{jt} + e_t^6$$

The variables in equation (6) are defined analogously to those in (4) and (5).

In estimating equations (4), (5), and (6), we assume that the wholesale price of gasoline at the Fairfax rack and the retail price are not jointly determined; i.e., $RACK_t$ is uncorrelated with the disturbance term in equations (4), (5), and (6).[36] One additional

_____

[36] In contrast to B&S, we do not instrument for rack prices. In our data, the rack price is the price of wholesale gasoline at the Fairfax , VA rack. Refiners supplying wholesale gasoline in Fairfax use pipelines connecting the major U.S. refining region in the Gulf to the major population centers on the eastern seaboard of the U.S. Refiners supplying Fairfax have the option of selling gasoline anywhere along the pipelines. Because gasoline demand in

complication in estimating equation (5) is that the error term appears to be non-stationary (the estimated autocorrelation coefficient is .99). Thus, we estimate equation (5) as a first difference to generate a stationary error, as shown in equation (5a) below. We can reject the null hypothesis of a unit root in equation (5a).[37]

$$(5a) \quad MARGIN_t - MARGIN_{t-1} = b_1(RACK_t - RACK_{t-1})$$
$$+ b_2(EXPECTED\ RACK_{t+1} - EXPECTED\ RACK_t)$$
$$+ b_3(\Delta RACK_t - \Delta RACK_{t-1}) + \sum_{j=1}^{11} D_j(M_{jt} - M_{jt-1}) + e_t - e_{t-1}$$

Table 7 presents the coefficient estimates for equations (5a) and (6). In contrast to B&S, the estimated impact of expected prices on current retail margins is sensitive to the specification of the lag process. The estimate from Model (5a) is similar to what B&S found: an increase in expected rack prices leads to a modest decrease in current retail margins. In contrast, the estimate from equation (6), which allows for a much more general lag process, finds essentially no effect of expected future rack prices on current retail margins. We interpret these findings as evidence that there are important dynamics in retail margins. However, because the test is very sensitive to model specification and because retail gasoline stations frequently change relative position in the price distribution, we conclude that conventional collusion models are unlikely to explain the observed changes in retail margins in our data.

5.4 History Dependent Demand/Asymmetric Price Adjustment

In order to examine asymmetric price adjustment as an explanation for changes in retail margins in our data, we follow Borenstein et al. (1997) and Bachmeier and Griffin (2003), in estimating the following equation:

Northern Virginia is a small fraction of U.S. gasoline demand, we treat the rack price as unaffected by demand in Northern Virginia.

[37] The Dickey-Fuller test statistic is 6.18 which implies the p-value corresponding to the rejecting the null hypothesis of a non-stationary disturbance is essentially zero. While equation (5a) does not include an intercept, we estimate it with an intercept that is effectively zero.

$$(7)\ \Delta RET_t = \sum_{k=0}^{2}\left(\beta_k^+ \Delta RACK_{t-k}^+ + \beta_i^- \Delta RACK_{t-k}^-\right) + \sum_{k=1}^{2}\left(\theta_k^+ \Delta RET_{t-k}^+ + \theta_k^- \Delta RET_{t-k}^-\right)$$

$$+\alpha_0(\text{Time Trend}_t) + [\delta_0 + \delta_1 RET_{t-1} + \delta_2 RACK_{t-1}] + \varepsilon_t$$

where the variables in equation (7) have the same definitions as those described in the previous subsection (i.e., equations (4), (5), and (6)). The motivation behind this specification is to allow retail prices to adjust asymmetrically in response to both changes in wholesale (rack) and previous retail prices changes. The term in brackets is defined as the error correction component of the estimating equation, which implicitly defines the long run relationship between retail and rack prices; that is, $\frac{\delta_2}{\delta_1}$ corresponds to the long-run pass thru rate between wholesale and retail prices.

There is some controversy about correctly estimating equation (7). Borenstein et al. estimate all of the parameters from equation (7) in one step. Bachmeier and Griffin (B&G) argue that a two step procedure is superior. In B&G's preferred approach, the error correction term is estimated in a first stage. The estimated coefficients from the error correction term are then imposed (as if they were estimated without error) and the remaining parameters are estimated in the second stage. We estimate models of asymmetric price adjustment using an estimation strategy very similar to both Borenstein et al. and B&G,[38] shown in columns 1 and 2, respectively, of Table 7.[39] Because the Borenstein et al. and B&G

---

[38] Following B&G's suggestion, we estimate their model by first estimating the cointegrating relationship (corresponding to the error correction term) using OLS. We use these parameter estimates to construct the error correction term. The error correction term is than imposed on the model (as if estimated without error) in estimating the remaining parameters in equation (6) by OLS and calculate Newey-West standard errors.

[39] Because we only have 3 years of weekly data for one city, it is not possible to include time dummies in our model as B&G and Borenstein et al. do. We have, however, included month of year dummies to control for seasonality in estimating equation (6). These coefficient estimates are not included for brevity, but are available on request.

estimation methods are very different, only the coefficients corresponding to the price adjustment terms shown in Table 7 are directly comparable.[40]

The parameter estimates corresponding to the price adjustment terms (the ΔRack_{t-k} and ΔRet_{t-k} terms) for the Borenstein et al. and B&G approaches are remarkably similar both in terms of the magnitudes and degrees of statistical precision. The estimated coefficients, however, are not economically plausible, or similar to the empirical results in either Borenstein et al. or B&G. For example, our estimates imply that wholesale price increases, *but not price decreases*, are passed through to retail. The estimated coefficient on the contemporaneous increase in wholesale price (ΔRACK_t^+) is estimated to be between .25 and .27, and is statistically significant. The estimated effect on a contemporaneous wholesale price decrease is never economically or statistically significant (less than .03 in absolute value). In contrast, Borenstein et al. and B&G find much larger effects of changes in wholesale prices on retail prices for both wholesale price increases and price decreases.[41] For this reason, we do not think a model of asymmetric price adjustment provides a good explanation for the changes in retail price we find in our data.[42]

---

[40] While both Borenstein et al. and B&G techniques are used to estimate essentially the same model (B&G do not include a time trend), a non-linear transformation is required to directly compare the parameter estimates corresponding to the intercept and the error correction terms of the two models.

[41] In all of the specifications B&G estimate, the contemporaneous effect of a change in upstream price on the downstream price is at least .75 (see Table 1, page 774). Borenstein et al., find large differences in the effect of contemporaneous wholesale price increases than decreases on retail prices, e.g., .62 vs. .2 in their Table 1, page 320, column 4. However, both papers find economically and statistically significant effects of decreases in wholesale price on retail price not seen in our data.

[42] Al-Gudhea et al. (2007) find sizeable asymmetry at the retail level. The asymmetry is most pronounced in the downstream portion of the distribution chain, the response of retail price to crude oil or wholesale gasoline price shocks. This asymmetry however lasts a matter of days and therefore does not explain the changes in retail margin we see in our data.

The last two columns of Table 7 include indicator variables corresponding to the years 1997 and 1998. For the B&G model we include these variables in the estimation of the cointegrating relationship, in Borenstein et al. we simply add them to equation (7). If these variables are economically significant, the implication is that the long-run margin is shifting between years. The estimates of B&G model suggest that the margins have changed. Here we see that long-run margins appear to shift down in both 1998 and 1999 relative to 1997. We interpret this evidence as suggesting that city-level margins appear to change by economically significant amounts over time.

5.5   Edgeworth Cycles

The most widely used test for Edgeworth cycles to date is the "eyeball test". The theoretical model predicts that retail stations' margins should have rapid increases followed by slower decreases. This leads to a pronounced saw-tooth pattern over time, which is particularly noticeable when wholesale prices are roughly constant; most empirical tests of cycle behavior are constructed largely with the goal of quantifying this test. Eckert and West (2003) suggests several possibilities, including: looking for asymmetry in the distribution of the length of "price runs"[43] and looking at the number of periods with little or no change in retail price (or margin). Lewis (2007) uses a threshold for the median daily price change. Eckert (2002) and Noel (2005, 2007b) offer more complex models of regime-switching to identify cycling, but this approach necessitates additional modeling assumptions regarding the behavior of prices under each regime. Thus, a finding of regime switching cannot be distinguished from a failure to correctly model the within-regime pricing behavior of the stations.

We employ several tests and find that our data are largely inconsistent with cycling behavior. First, as can be seen in Figure 1, the characteristic saw-tooth pattern indicative of cycling is not readily apparent. While there are some short-term fluctuations in margins, these are all on the order of one to three cents and do not explain the larger fluctuations. The larger fluctuations are too long-lived to be consistent with cycling. The existing literature has typically found cycles measured in hours or weeks, not months. Second, the Markov

---

[43] A "price run" is defined as a set of weeks with consecutive same-sign price changes.

transition matrices in Figure 6 are not consistent with cycling behavior. The theory of cycling behavior (both symmetric and asymmetric) predicts that while stations might be relenting or undercutting, they do not leave their margins unchanged. Thus, there should be very little mass on the diagonal. This is not consistent with what we observe: that stations residuals are most likely to remain where they were in the previous week, and that there is very little mass in the upper left and lower right corners.

6.0   Discussion and Conclusion

We examined weekly pricing for three years in the late 1990s of 272 stations in Northern Virginia. Our main finding is that gasoline stations do not appear to follow simple static pricing rules. Gasoline stations do not charge constant margins, nor do they simply maintain the same relative position in the pricing distribution. We find from week-to-week, gas stations are more likely than not to change their relative position in the pricing distribution (measured relative to a regional price or rank among nearby stations). There is also heterogeneity in stations' pricing behavior over time. Stations that charge very high prices or very low prices in one week are much more likely to charge high or low prices in subsequent weeks than stations charging prices near the mean. There is also an interesting asymmetry in this behavior: low priced stations are much more likely to remain low priced than high priced stations are to remain high. While most week-to-week changes in pricing position are small, a significant number of stations make large changes in their pricing. For example, 24% of stations change their relative position in the pricing distribution by more than 25 percentage points between 1998 and 1999.

We believe our most interesting finding is that retail margins change sizably over time. For example, for a six month period the implied retail mark-up (retail price less taxes and wholesale prices) is roughly 19 cents for 6 months and then falls to about 10 cents for 3 months. The evidence suggests the entire distribution is shifting over time, not just the median or mean. In a market with little entry or exit, little non-geographic differentiation, where wholesale prices are observable with little brand variation in rack prices and inelastic demand, one would expect more constant retail margins. The explanation that prices reflect coordinated behavior (e.g., tacit collusion followed by periodic price wars), is also difficult to accept. In both high and low margin periods, gasoline stations continuously change their relative positions in the pricing distribution. Hence, these models predict that the market would always be in the penalty phase. Further, tacit collusion would appear unlikely in Northern Virginia given the low level of concentration at the retail level – there are roughly *25* different brands of retail gasoline in Northern Virginia.[44] This finding is worthy of further investigation. More generally, many of our results can be interpreted as adding to mounting evidence, e.g., Eckert and West (2003, 2004a, 2004b), Noel (2007a, 2007b) and Slade (1992), that localized retail gasoline competition appears to be characterized by regime shifts in pricing.

We have also examined how our empirical findings relate to existing theories of pricing that appear most relevant for retail gasoline. While each of these theories explains some aspects of gasoline pricing, none provide explanations for the pricing dynamics we observe. Given the explosion in the quantity of data available for studying retail gasoline markets, we view retail gasoline markets as a promising area for future research. We hope that our empirical findings can provide useful guidance for future work on modeling retail gasoline pricing behavior.

_____

[44] Because most branded stations are operated independent of the refiner, this understates the number of independent price-setting agents. Most stations in our data are operated by a lessee dealer (an individual who leases the station from the refiner) or a jobber (a franchisee that owns the station.) The lessee dealer or jobber sets the retail price, not the refiner.

References

Al-Gudhea, S., Kenc, T. and S. Dibooglu, 2007, "Do Retail Gasoline Prices Rise More Readily Than They Fall? A Threshold Cointegration Approach.," *Journal of Economics and Business*, v. 59, pp. 560-574.

Athey, S. and K. Bagwell, 2001, "Optimal Collusion with Private Information," *The RAND Journal of Economics*, v. 32, pp.428-465.

Athey, S., K. Bagwell, and C. Sanchirico, 2004, "Collusion and Price Rigidity," *Review of Economic Studies*, v. 71, pp. 317-349.

Bachmeier, L. and J. Griffin, 2003, "New Evidence on Asymmetric Gasoline Price Responses," *The Review of Economics and Statistics*, v. 85, pp.772-776.

Barron, J., B. Taylor, and Umbeck, J., 2000, "A Theory of Quality-Related Differences in Retail Margins: Why There is a Premium on Premium Gasoline," *Economic Inquiry*, 38 (4), 550-569.

Barron, J., B. Taylor, and Umbeck, J., 2004, "Number of Sellers, Average Prices and Price Dispersion," *International Journal of Industrial Organization,* v. 22 pp. 1041-66.

Baye, M, D. Kovenock and C. G. DeVries, 1992, "It Takes Two to Tango: Equilibrium in a Model of Sales," *Games and Economic Behavior*, 4, pp. 493-510.

Borenstein, S., A. Cameron, and R. Gilbert, 1997, "Do Gasoline Prices Respond Asymmetrically to Crude Oil Price Changes," *Quarterly Journal of Economics*, v. 112, pp. 305-339.

Borenstein, S., A. Shepard, 1986, "Dynamic Pricing in Retail Gasoline Markets," *The RAND Journal of Economics*, v. 27, pp. 429-251.

Conlisk, J., Gerstner, E., and Sobel, J., 1984, "Cyclic Pricing by a Durable Goods Monopolist," *Quarterly Journal of Economics* v. 99, pp. 489-505.

Eckert, A, 2002, "Retail Price Cycles and Response Asymmetry," *The Canadian Journal of Economics*, v. 35, pp. 52-77.

Eckert, A. and D. West, 2003, "Retail Price Cycles and the Presence of Small Firms," *International Journal of Industrial Organization*, v. 21, pp. 151-170.

Eckert, A. and D. West, 2004a, "Retail Gasoline Price Cycles across Spatially Dispersed Gasoline Stations," *Journal of Law and Economics*, v. 47, pp. 245-73.

Eckert, A. and D. West, 2004b, "A Tale of Two Cities: Price Uniformity and Price

Volatility in Gasoline Retailing," *Annals of Regional Science*, v. 38, pp. 25-46.

Federal Trade Commission, 2004, *The Petroleum Industry: Mergers, Structural Change, and Antitrust Enforcement.*

Federal Trade Commission, 2006. *Investigation of Gasoline Price Manipulation and Post-Katrina Gasoline Price Increases.*

Galeotti, M., A. Lanza and M. Manera, 2003, "Rockets and Feathers Revisited: An International Comparison on European Gasoline Markets," *Energy Economics* V. 25 pp. 175-190.

Green, E. and R. Porter, 1984, "Noncooperative Collusion Under Imperfect Price Competition," *Econometrica* v. 52 pp.87-100.

Haltiwanger, J, J. Harrington, 1991, "The Impact of Cyclical Demand Movements on Collusive Behavior", *RAND Journal of Economics*, v. 22, pp. 89-106.

Hastings, J., 2004, "Vertical Relationships and Competition in Retail Gasoline Markets: Empirical Evidence from Contract Changes in Southern California," *American Economic Review*, 94(1), pp. 317-328.

Hoch S., X. Dreze, and M. Purk, 1994., "The EDLP, High Low and Margin Arithmetic", *Journal of Marketing*, 58: 16-27.

Hong, P, R. P. McAfee, and A. Nayyar, 2002, "Equilibrium Price Dispersion with Consumer Inventories" *Journal of Economic Theory*, 105, pp. 503-517.

Hosken, D. and D. Reiffen, 2004, "How do Retailers Determine Sale Products: Evidence from Store-Level Data," *Journal of Consumer Policy*, 27, pp.141-177.

Lal, R. and C. Matutes, 1994, "Retail Pricing and Advertising Strategies," *Journal of Business*, 67, pp. 345-70.

Lach, S., 2002, "Existence and Persistence of Price Dispersion: An Empirical Analysis," *Review of Economics and Statistics*, 84(3), pp. 433–444

Lewis, M., 2005a, "Asymmetric Price Adjustment and Consumer Search: An Examination of the Retail Gas Market," working paper.

Lewis, M., 2005b, "Is Price Dispersion a Sign of Competition," working paper.

Lewis, M, 2007, "Temporary Wholesale Gasoline Price Spikes Have Long-lasting Retail Effects: The Aftermath of Hurricane Rita," working paper.

Manuszak, M., 2002, "The Impact of Upstream Mergers on Retail Gasoline Prices," working paper.

Maskin, E. and J. Tirole, 1988, "A Theory of Dynamic Oligopoly, II: Price Competition, Kinked Demand Curves, and Edgeworth Cycles," *Econometrica*, v. 56, pp. 571-99.

Meyer, D. and J. Fischer, 2004, "The Economics of Price Zones and Territorial Restrictions in Gasoline Marketing," *Federal Trade Commission Bureau of Economics Working Paper #271.*

Noel, M., 2007a, "Edgeworth Price Cycles, Cost-Based Pricing and Sticky Pricing in Retail Gasoline Markets," *Review of Economics and Statistics*, forthcoming.

Noel, M., 2007b, "Edgeworth Price Cycles: Evidence from the Toronto Retail Gasoline Market," *Journal of Industrial Economics*, forthcoming.

Noel, M., 2005, "Edgeworth Price Cycles and Focal Prices: Computational Dynamic Markov Equilibria," working paper.

Pashigian, B, 1988, "Demand Uncertainty and Sales: A Study of Fashion and Markdown Pricing," *American Economic Review*, 78, pp. 936-53.

Pashigian, B. and B. Bowen, 1991, "Why are Products Sold on Sales?: Explanations of Pricing Regularities," *Quarterly Journal of Economics* v. 106, pp.1014-1038.

Pesendorfer, M., 2002, "Retail Sales: A Study of Pricing Behavior in Super Markets," *Journal of Business*, v. 75, pp.33-66.

Porter, R., 1985, "On the Incidence and Duration of Price Wars," *Journal of Industrial Economics*, v 33, pp. 415-426.

Rotemberg, J. and G. Saloner, 1986, "A Supergame-Theoretic Model of Price Wars During Booms," *American Economic Review*, v. 76, pp.390-407.

Shepard, A., 1990, "Pricing Behavior and Vertical Contracts in Retail Markets," *American Economics Association Papers and Proceedings*, 80(2), 427-431.

Shepard, A., 1991, "Price Discrimination and Retail Configuration," *Journal of Political Economy*, 99(11), 30-53.

Shepard, A., 1993, "Contractual Form, Retail Price, and Asset Characteristics in Gasoline Retailing," *RAND Journal of Economics*, 24(1), 58-77.

Slade, M., 1987, "Interfirm Rivalry in a Repeated Game: An Empirical Test of Tacit Collusion," *The Journal of Industrial Economics*, v. 35, pp.499-515.

Slade, M., 1992, "Vancouver's Gasoline-Price Wars: An Empirical Exercise in Uncovering Supergame Strategies," *Review of Economic Studies*, 59, 257-276.

Thomadsen, R., 2005, "The Effect of Ownership Structure on Prices in Geographically Differentiated Industries," *The RAND Journal of Economics*, v. 36, pp.908-929.

White, H. (1982) "Maximum Likelihood Estimation of Misspecified Models" *Econometrica*, v. 50 1-25.

Varian, H.R. (1980) "A Model of Sales," *American Economic Review*; 70, pp. 651-9.

Table 1: Descriptive Statistics for OPIS Sample and Census

	Minimum	Maximum	Mean (StdDev) OPIS Sample	Mean (StdDev) Census
Continuous Variables:				
Retail Price (cents)	71.9	145.9	111.45	n/a
Std Dev			11.35	
Number of Gas Stations within 1.5 miles	0	10	8.62	8.30
Std Dev			2.66	2.83
Distance to Closest Gas Station (miles)	0.002	3.08	0.21	0.20
Std Dev			0.34	0.42
Fraction of Mobil and Exxon Stations Nearby	0	1	0.36	0.35
Std Dev			0.16	0.18
Fraction of Low-Priced Stations Nearby	0	0.4	0.04	0.05
Std Dev			0.07	0.08
Fraction of Lessee Dealer Stations Nearby	0	0.9	0.51	0.46
Std Dev			0.18	0.20
Fraction of Company Owned and Operated Stations Nearby	0	0.6	0.11	0.13
Std Dev			0.11	0.13
Number of Pumps	1	16	7.69	7.28
Std Dev			2.85	3.31
Population in Zip Code	1377	62132	30393.73	29658.97
Std Dev			12467.93	12389.33
Population Density in Zip Code	131.4	12305.9	4423.13	4271.787
Std Dev			2793.66	2888.824
Median Family Income in Zip Code	37304	154817	72002.68	73284.14
Std Dev			18195.71	20082.67
Median Household Commuting Time in Zip Code (minutes)	22	42	30.70	30.36
Std Dev			3.91	4.28
Indicator Variables:				
Convenience Store			0.05	0.07
Provides Repair Service			0.62	0.56
Outdated Format			0.24	0.29
Self Serve Only			0.84	0.74
Ownership Type:				
Lessee Dealer			0.58	0.46
Jobber Owned			0.08	0.09
Company Owned and Operated			0.14	0.13
Open Dealer			0.21	0.27
Year=1997			36.19	
Year=1998			31.74	
Year=1999			32.07	
Number of Observations (station-weeks)			27,853	570

Table 2: Comparison of Brand Distribution In New Image Marketing Census and OPIS Sample

Brand	OPIS Sample		New Image Census
	Percent of Station-Weeks	Percent of Stations	Percent of Stations
Amoco	0.00	0.00	9.3
Blue Max	0.00	0.00	0.18
BP	0.4	1.14	1.05
Chevron	0.66	2.27	1.75
Citgo	10.31	15.91	11.58
Coastal	0.05	0.38	0.7
Crown	7.19	5.68	3.16
Dixie	0.00	0.00	0.35
Eagle	0.00	0.00	0.18
Exxon	0.00	0.00	22.11
Gas King	0.00	0.00	0.18
Getty	0.71	0.76	0.7
Global	0.00	0.00	0.18
Hess	0.75	1.52	1.93
JAC	0.00	0.00	0.18
Merit	0.42	0.76	0.35
Mobil	27.62	23.86	14.39
Quarles	0.00	0.00	0.53
Racetrac	0.00	0.00	0.18
Sheetz	0.27	0.38	0.53
Shell	23.71	21.21	11.23
Sunoco	5.31	6.06	3.33
Texaco	22.27	19.32	10
Wawa	0.00	0.00	0.18
Xtra Fuels	0.33	0.75	0.7
Unbranded	0.00	0.00	5.09

Table 3: Regressions of Retail Margin on Station Characteristics And Time Indicators
(All Stations)

	Pooled		1997		1998		1999	
	Coefficient	T-Statistic	Coefficient	T-Statistic	Coefficient	T-Statistic	Coefficient	T-Statistic
Company Owned and Operated	1.52	2.13	1.02	1.72	1.72	1.80	1.50	1.48
Lessee Dealer	0.53	1.40	0.46	1.08	0.41	0.91	0.76	1.60
Fraction of Lessee Dealer Stations Nearby	-0.49	-0.59	-0.28	-0.35	-0.15	-0.13	-0.97	-0.93
Fraction of Company Owned and Operated Stations Nearby	-0.31	-0.21	0.10	0.07	-0.76	-0.37	-0.19	-0.09
Fraction of Mobil and Exxon Stations Nearby	0.11	0.11	1.22	1.41	-0.35	-0.24	-1.20	-0.84
Fraction of Low-Priced Stations Nearby	1.48	0.65	-2.98	-1.66	2.75	0.80	4.22	1.16
Number of Gas Stations within 1.5 miles	-0.04	-0.60	-0.03	-0.40	-0.04	-0.46	-0.08	-0.95
Distance to Closest Gas Station (miles)	0.43	0.65	0.97	1.98	0.20	0.24	-0.16	-0.20
Convenience Store	-0.81	-1.28	-0.29	-0.39	-0.14	-0.17	-0.46	-0.54
Provides Repair Service	0.92	2.63	0.68	2.30	1.40	3.04	1.00	2.18
Outdated Format	0.63	1.89	0.28	0.60	0.67	1.72	0.79	1.79
Self Serve Only	-0.05	-0.71	-0.05	-0.99	-0.06	-0.68	-0.01	-0.14
Number of Pumps	0.40	1.09	-0.04	-0.08	1.32	2.74	0.32	0.61
Log of Population in Zip Code	-1.50	-3.81	-0.72	-2.75	-1.68	-3.54	-2.00	-3.58
Log of Population Density in Zip Code	0.75	3.65	-0.20	-1.03	1.18	4.08	1.58	5.20
Log of Median Income in Zip Code	1.57	2.56	0.08	0.13	2.13	2.48	3.19	3.62
Log of Median Travel Time	-5.17	-4.85	-0.28	-0.35	-8.73	-5.43	-7.85	-5.30
Station Fixed Effects (Citgo Omitted)								
BP	2.37	1.65	3.53	2.64	-1.65	-2.35	n/a	
Chevron	-2.94	-2.68	-2.46	-2.04	-6.58	-9.19	-0.65	-0.67
Coastal	-9.79	-12.05	-11.58	-13.20	n/a		n/a	
Crown	-4.54	-5.58	-4.22	-5.15	-5.39	-4.97	-3.66	-3.23
Getty	-0.34	-0.36	0.47	0.23	-1.65	-1.88	-1.00	-1.07
Hess	-4.39	-4.60	-1.93	-1.32	-5.74	-4.81	-4.77	-3.83
Kenyon	-0.53	-0.90	n/a		-2.00	-2.72	n/a	
Merit	-2.78	-2.37	n/a		-5.45	-5.26	-2.75	-2.18
Mobil	0.14	0.25	1.62	2.27	-1.09	-1.56	-0.40	-0.51
Sheetz	-5.81	-5.56	n/a		-5.83	-4.23	-4.32	-2.90
Shell	0.87	1.68	1.37	2.05	-0.05	-0.07	1.10	1.45
Sunoco	-2.88	-4.12	-1.61	-2.16	-4.22	-5.19	-3.43	-3.31
Texaco	2.01	4.08	2.57	3.84	0.96	1.48	2.20	3.16
Xtra Fuels	-1.30	-1.76	-1.74	-2.26	-0.51	-0.54	n/a	
Constant	59.74	6.34	58.97	6.49	71.28	5.27	47.37	3.56
Number of Observations (station-weeks)	27853		10073		8835		8927	
R-squared	0.66		0.67		0.68		0.63	

Notes: The Retail Margin is defined as the retail price less the branded rack, the omitted station brand is Citgo, the omitted ownership types are jobber and open dealers, standard errors clustered by station, and each specification includes week dummies (not shown).

Table 4: Regressions of Retail Margin on Station Characteristics and Time Indicators (Non-Crown Stations)

	Pooled		1997		1998		1999	
	Coefficient	T-Statistic	Coefficient	T-Statistic	Coefficient	T-Statistic	Coefficient	T-Statistic
Company Owned and Operated	1.63	2.15	1.05	1.65	1.87	1.84	1.61	1.48
Lessee Dealer	0.55	1.44	0.50	1.15	0.40	0.88	0.77	1.62
Fraction of Lessee Dealer Stations Nearby	-0.91	-1.06	-0.54	-0.66	-0.56	-0.49	-1.52	-1.38
Fraction of Company Owned and Operated Stations Nearby	-0.11	-0.07	0.15	0.09	-0.44	-0.21	0.11	0.05
Fraction of Mobil and Exxon Stations Nearby	-0.14	-0.13	1.26	1.37	-0.78	-0.52	-1.67	-1.10
Fraction of Low-Priced Stations Nearby	0.59	0.25	-3.52	-1.78	1.63	0.45	3.17	0.84
Number of Gas Stations within 1.5 miles	-0.04	-0.54	-0.02	-0.39	-0.03	-0.34	-0.08	-0.94
Distance to Closest Gas Station (miles)	1.47	2.72	1.55	2.73	1.56	2.02	1.02	1.53
Convenience Store	-1.03	-1.68	-0.38	-0.52	-0.44	-0.56	-0.71	-0.87
Provides Repair Service	0.53	2.65	0.70	2.36	1.38	3.01	1.00	2.14
Outdated Format	0.48	1.50	0.21	0.45	0.47	1.27	0.60	1.39
Self Serve Only	-0.08	-1.21	-0.05	-1.13	-0.12	-1.35	-0.06	-0.56
Number of Pumps	0.55	1.52	0.00	0.01	1.60	3.30	0.50	0.96
Log of Population in Zip Code	-1.50	-3.72	-0.74	-2.69	-1.71	-3.47	-1.96	-3.41
Log of Population Density in Zip Code	0.74	3.49	-0.19	-0.94	1.15	3.79	1.54	4.90
Log of Median Income in Zip Code	1.68	2.52	-0.02	-0.02	2.43	2.59	3.37	3.56
Log of Median Travel Time	-4.79	-4.50	-0.08	-0.10	-8.29	-5.22	-7.43	-4.86
Station Fixed Effects (Citgo Omitted)								
BP	2.25	1.61	3.47	2.43	-1.48	-2.11	n/a	
Chevron	-2.85	-2.48	-2.32	-1.80	-6.65	-9.64	-0.50	-0.51
Coastal	-10.06	-12.14	-11.59	-12.96	n/a		n/a	
Crown	n/a		n/a		n/a		n/a	
Getty	-0.06	-0.06	0.65	0.32	-1.26	-1.47	-0.60	-0.62
Hess	-4.30	-4.30	-1.80	-1.16	-5.63	-4.53	-4.70	-3.56
Kenyon	-0.57	-0.94	n/a		-2.12	-2.83	n/a	
Merit	-2.70	-2.40	n/a		-5.31	-5.00	-2.68	-2.14
Mobil	0.17	0.28	1.62	2.25	-1.00	-1.43	-0.38	-0.47
Sheetz	-5.30	-5.15	n/a		-5.03	-3.78	-3.72	-2.51
Shell	0.55	1.80	1.37	2.04	0.11	0.18	1.22	1.57
Sunoco	-2.67	-3.86	-1.52	-2.02	-3.90	-4.97	-3.16	-3.06
Texaco	2.05	4.06	2.56	3.81	1.06	1.63	2.26	3.18
Xtra Fuels	-0.74	-1.01	-1.52	-1.90	0.33	0.35	n/a	
Constant	57.59	5.84	59.38	6.09	67.24	4.74	47.31	3.46
Number of Observations (station-weeks)	25,883		9,278		8,194		8,134	
R-squared	0.65		0.63		0.67		0.62	

Notes: The Retail Margin is defined as the retail price less the branded rack, the omitted station brand is Citgo, the omitted ownership types are jobber and open dealers, standard errors clustered by station, and each specification includes week dummies (not shown).

Table 5: Change In Relative Position of Gas Station Fixed Effects in Frequency Distribution Between Years

	1997 to 1998	1998 to 1999	1997 to 1999
Change in Relative Distribution of:			
10+ Percentage Points	52%	35%	67%
15+ Percentage Points	37%	21%	52%
20+ Percentage Points	25%	13%	40%
25+ Percentage Points	16%	10%	27%
50+ Percentage Points	4%	2%	6%
75+ Percentage Points	1%	1%	1%

Notes: This table analyzes the changes over time in the estimated station-level fixed effects from regressions of margins on weeks and station fixed effects estimated separtately by year. This table examines how station-level fixed effects change between years by examining where in the frequency distribution a station's fixed effect falls between two years. For example, 4% of gasoline stations experienced a dramatic change in their relative price between 1997 and 1998, changing by 50 percentage points, e.g., moving from the 25th percentile to the 75th percentile.

Table 6: Change In Relative Size of Gas Station Fixed Effects Between Years In Cents

	1997 to 1998	1998 to 1999	1997 to 1999
Percent of Statistically Significant Changes (z-	33%	27%	45%
Mean Size of Change (in cents, conditional on being significant)	3.82	2.76	3.84
Number of Comparisons	170	193	163

Notes: This table presents the magnitude of changes in a station's relative margin between years conditional on the change in a station's margin being statistically significant. For example, between 1997 and 1998 33% of station's changed their average margin (measured relative to the average margin in northern Virginia) by a statistically significant amount. Conditional on the change being statistically significant, the mean change in relative margin was 3.82 cents.

Table 7: Test of Borenstein and Shepard (1996)
Estimation of Margin Equation

Variable	Equation (5a)		Equation (6)	
	Coefficient	T-Statistic	Coefficient	T-Statistic
EXPECTED RACK$_{t+1}$	-0.397	-2.500	-0.002	-0.030
RACK$_t$	-0.194	-2.620	n/a	n/a
ΔRACK$_t$	-0.490	-3.890	n/a	n/a
RACK$_{t-1}$	n/a	n/a	-0.918	-13.230
RET$_{t-1}$	n/a	n/a	0.923	52.910
ΔRACK^+_t	n/a	n/a	-0.759	-11.030
ΔRACK$^+_{t-1}$	n/a	n/a	0.165	1.730
ΔRACK$^+_{t-2}$	n/a	n/a	-0.028	-0.560
ΔRACK^-_t	n/a	n/a	-1.007	-25.950
ΔRACK$^-_{t-1}$	n/a	n/a	0.027	0.480
ΔRACK$^-_{t-2}$	n/a	n/a	-0.066	-1.890
ΔRET$^+_{t-1}$	n/a	n/a	0.438	2.390
ΔRET$^+_{t-2}$	n/a	n/a	0.097	0.810
ΔRET$^-_{t-1}$	n/a	n/a	0.404	2.680
ΔRET$^-_{t-2}$	n/a	n/a	0.042	0.320
Constant	0.006	0.060	0.651	1.910
Observations	150		150	
Estimation Method	OLS, Newey-West Standard Errors		OLS, Newey-West Standard Errors	

Note: Dependent Variable is the average retail margin in our sample in week t (RET$_t$ - RACK$_t$). RACK$_t$ is the Fairfax branded rack price in week t, RET$_t$ is the average retail price of gasoline in Northern Virginia in week t, ΔRack$_t$=Rack$_t$-Rack$_{t-1}$, ΔRET$_t$=RET$_t$-RET$_{t-1}$., ΔRET$^+$t=ΔRET$_t$ if ΔRET>0, ΔRET$^-_{t-1}$=ΔRET$_{t-1}$ if ΔRET$_{t-1}$<0. ΔRACK+t-1 and ΔRACK-t-1 are defined analagously. Equation (5a) is estimated as a first difference. The estimating equations also include 11 monthly indicator variables.

Table 8: Estimation of Asymmetric Price Adjustment Models

	Borenstein et al.		Bachmeier and Griffin		Borenstein et al.		Bachmeier and Griffin	
Primary Equation	Coefficient	T-statistic	Coefficient	T-statistic	Coefficient	T-statistic	Coefficient	T-statistic
Constant	3.898	3.670	-0.702	-1.780	5.022	2.370	-0.679	-1.830
$\Delta RACK^+_t$	0.256	3.530	0.268	3.810	0.246	3.250	0.269	3.840
$\Delta RACK^+_{t-1}$	0.165	1.900	0.248	2.700	0.157	1.870	0.249	2.700
$\Delta RACK^+_{t-2}$	-0.022	-0.470	0.031	0.620	-0.023	-0.500	0.031	0.620
$\Delta RACK^-_t$	-0.001	-0.020	-0.031	-0.750	-0.005	-0.120	-0.030	-0.740
$\Delta RACK^-_{t-1}$	0.023	0.460	0.073	1.450	0.019	0.370	0.073	1.460
$\Delta RACK^-_{t-2}$	-0.066	-1.880	-0.016	-0.430	-0.072	-2.110	-0.016	-0.430
ΔRET^+_{t-1}	0.432	2.340	0.416	2.260	0.426	2.230	0.415	2.270
ΔRET^+_{t-2}	0.104	0.940	0.122	0.900	0.096	0.880	0.124	0.910
ΔRET^-_{t-1}	0.409	2.700	0.525	3.700	0.384	2.580	0.528	3.730
ΔRET^-_{t-2}	0.063	0.470	0.209	1.510	0.046	0.340	0.212	1.530
$RACK_{t-1}$	0.084	5.050	n/a	n/a	0.087	5.160	n/a	n/a
RET_{t-1}	-0.081	-4.680	n/a	n/a	-0.088	-4.800	n/a	n/a
Time	-0.001	-0.860	n/a	n/a	-0.010	-0.300	n/a	n/a
Year=1998	n/a	n/a	n/a	n/a	0.317	0.180	n/a	n/a
Year=1999	n/a	n/a	n/a	n/a	0.927	0.270	n/a	n/a
Error Correction Term	n/a	n/a	0.003	0.810	n/a	n/a	0.003	0.820
Cointegrating Relationship								
Constant	n/a	n/a	56.00	32.24	n/a	n/a	63.22	27.89
$Rack_{t-1}$	n/a	n/a	0.93	32.16	n/a	n/a	0.85	25.78
Year=1998	n/a	n/a	n/a	n/a	n/a	n/a	-3.41	-3.99
Year=1999	n/a	n/a	n/a	n/a	n/a	n/a	-4.86	-6.95
Observations	151		151		151		151	
Estimation Method	OLS, Newey West Standard Errors		OLS, Newey West Standard Errors		OLS, Newey West Standard Errors		OLS, Newey West Standard Errors	

Note: $Rack_t$ is the Fairfax branded rack price in week t, Ret_t is the average retail price of gasoline in Northern Virginia in week t, $\Delta Rack_t = Rack_t - Rack_{t-1}$, and $\Delta Ret_t = Ret_t - Ret_{t-1}$, all specifications include month indicator variables (not shown).

Figure 1: Weekly Retail Gasoline Margins and Branded Rack Prices
1997-1999

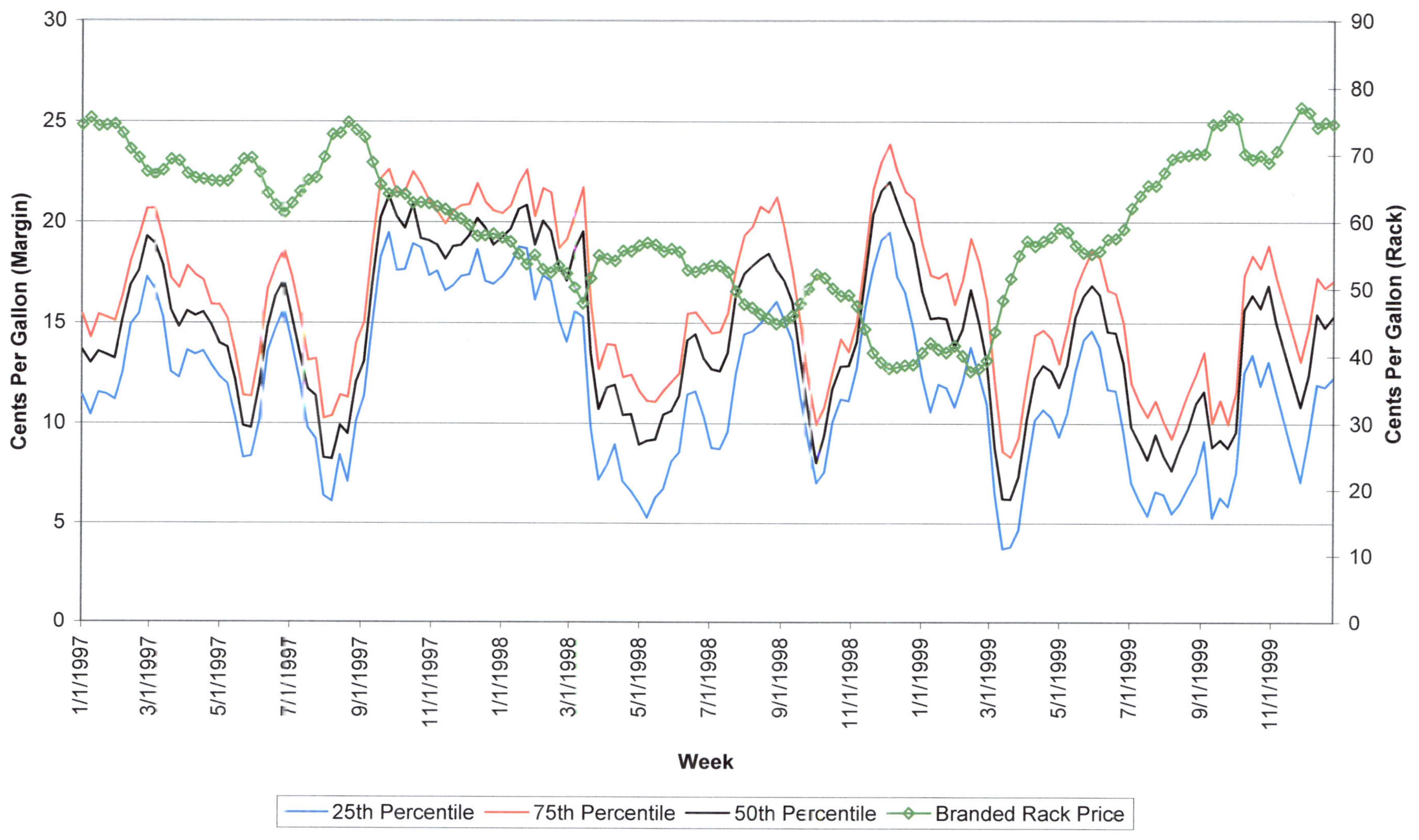

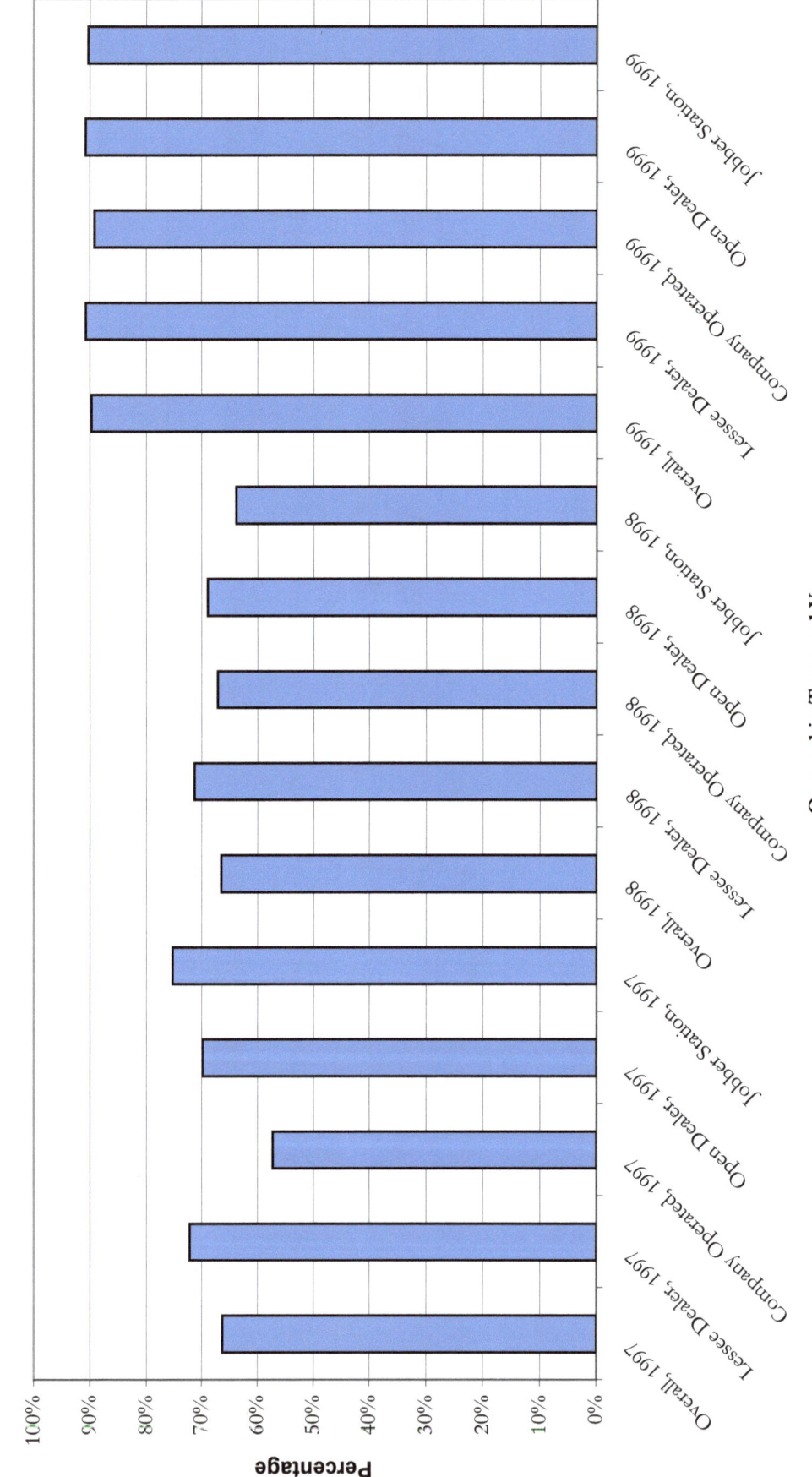

Figure 2: Percentage of Retail Price Variation Generated by Time Series Variation Overall and By Station Ownership Type
(Within Variation)

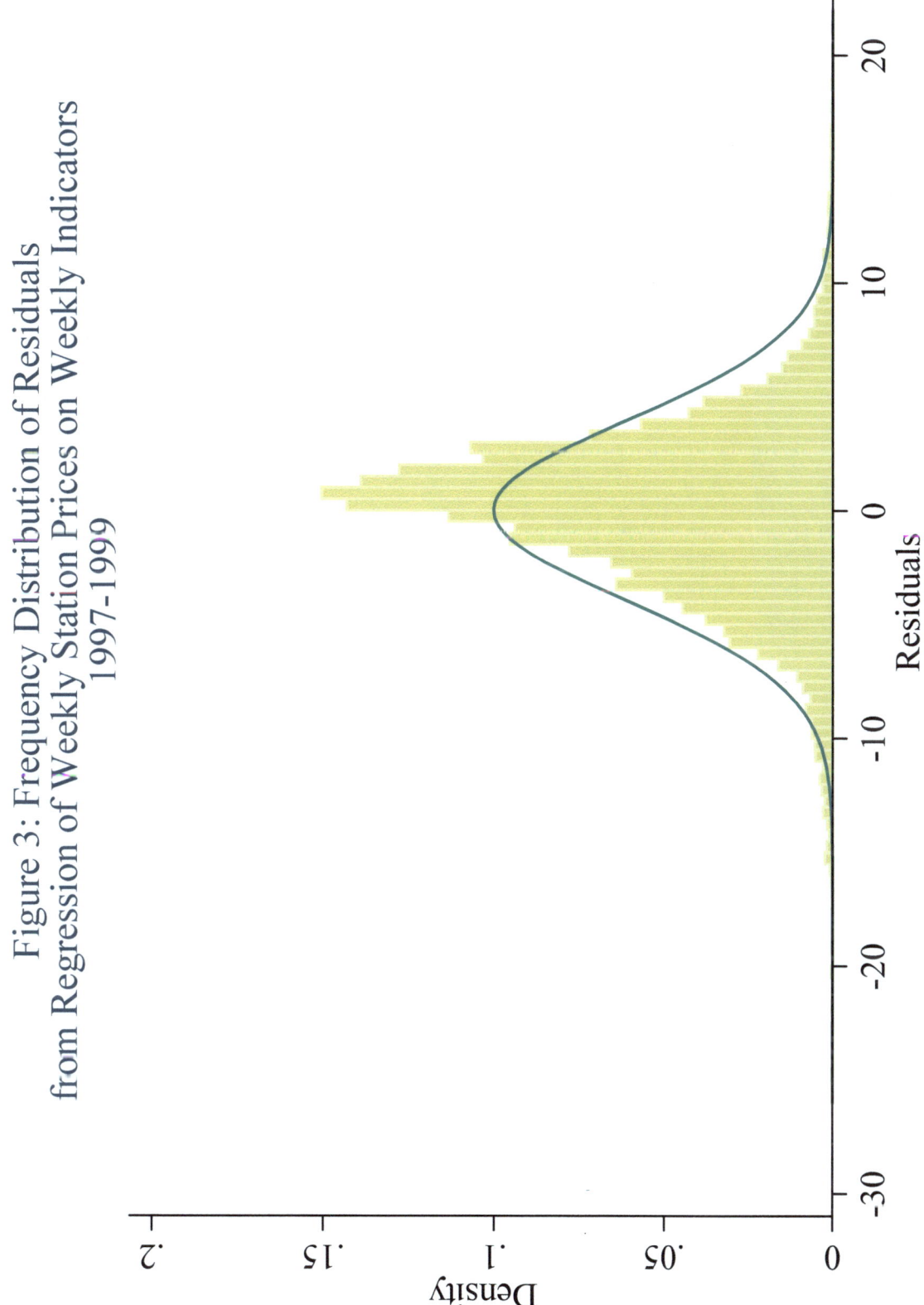

Figure 3: Frequency Distribution of Residuals
from Regression of Weekly Station Prices on Weekly Indicators
1997-1999

Figure 4: Single-Period Empirical Markov Transition Matrix
Relative Price in Current Week Conditional on Relative Price In Previous Week
Residuals from Regression of Price on Week Indicators

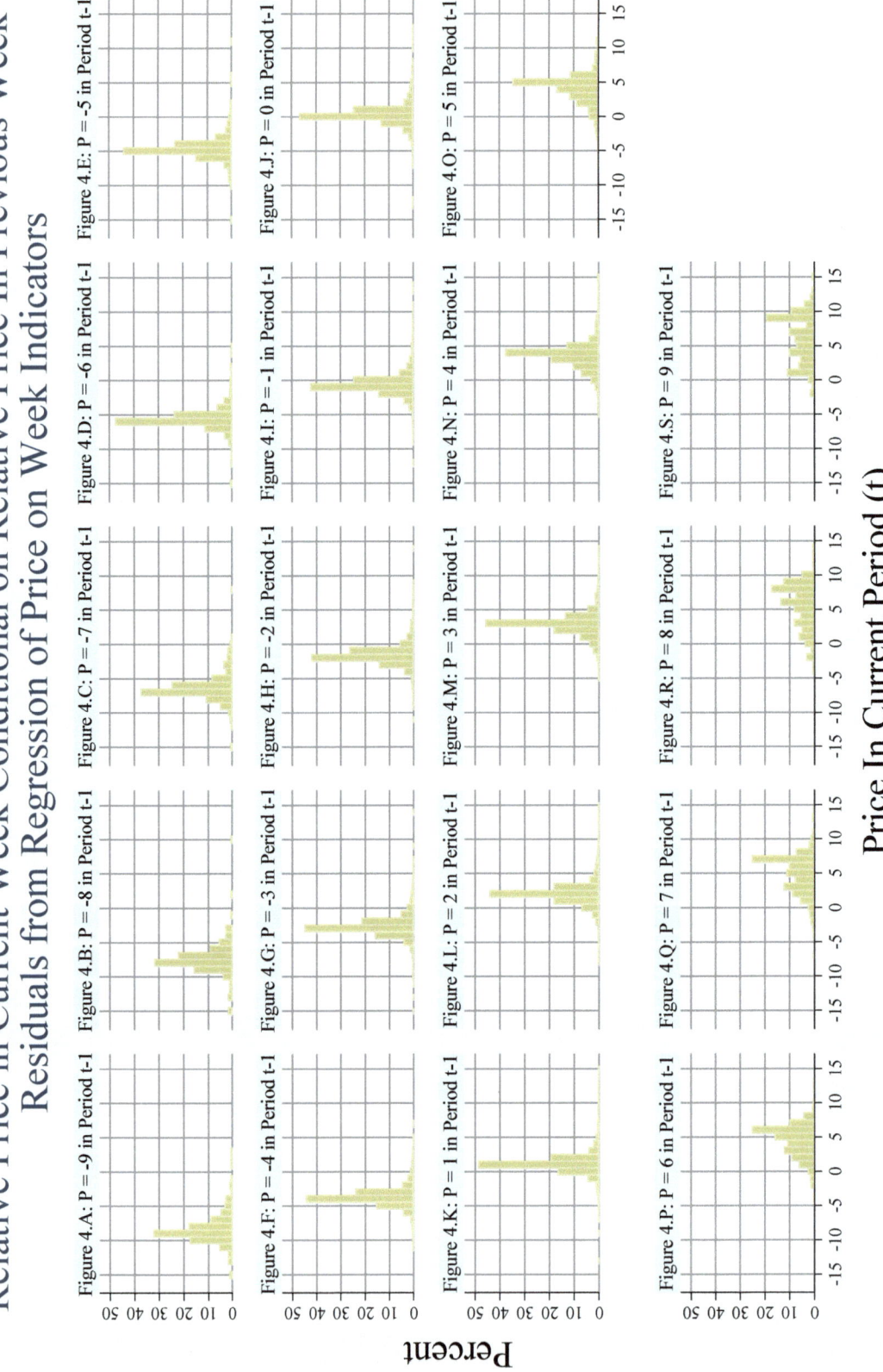

Price In Current Period (t)

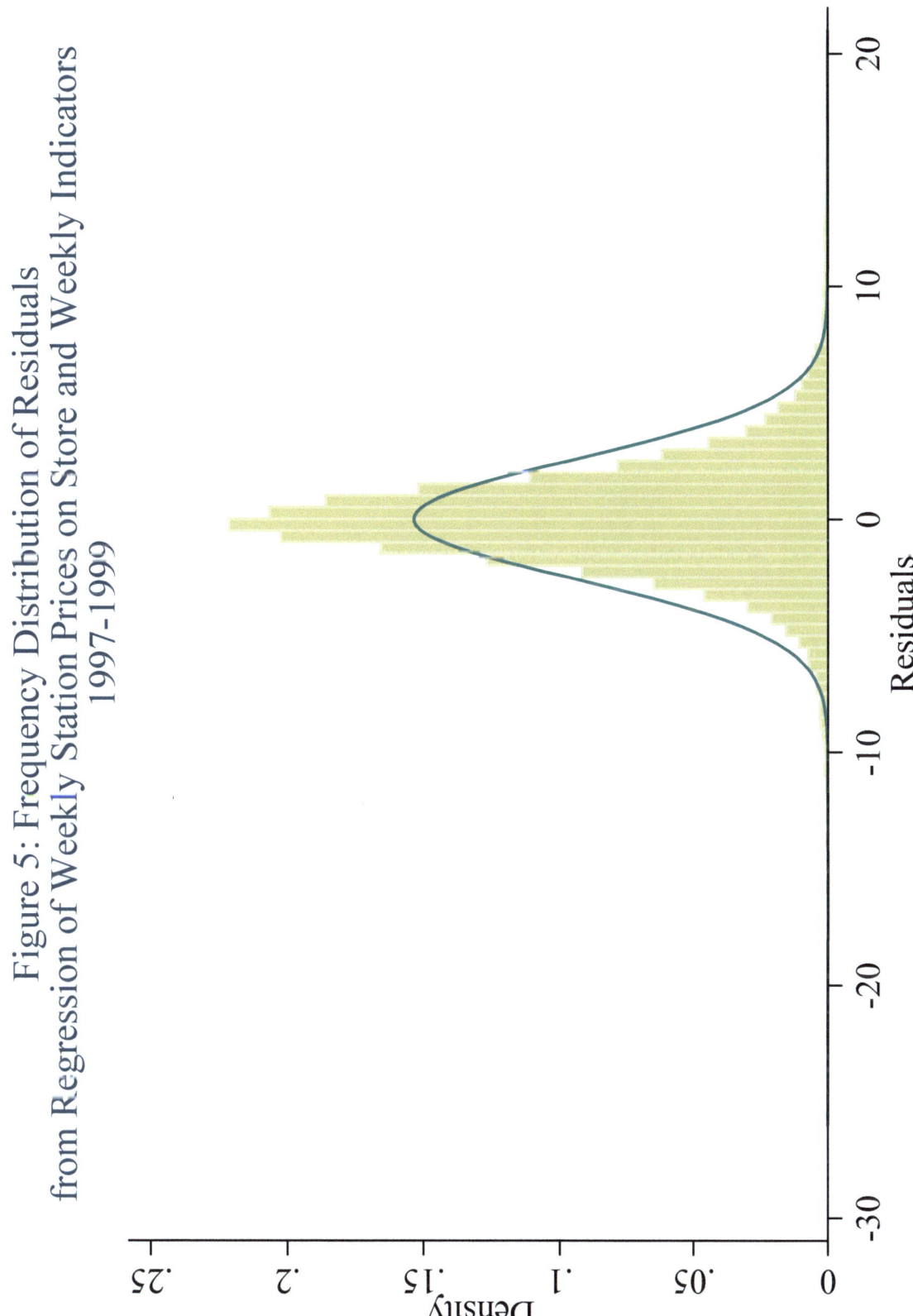

Figure 5: Frequency Distribution of Residuals
from Regression of Weekly Station Prices on Store and Weekly Indicators
1997-1999

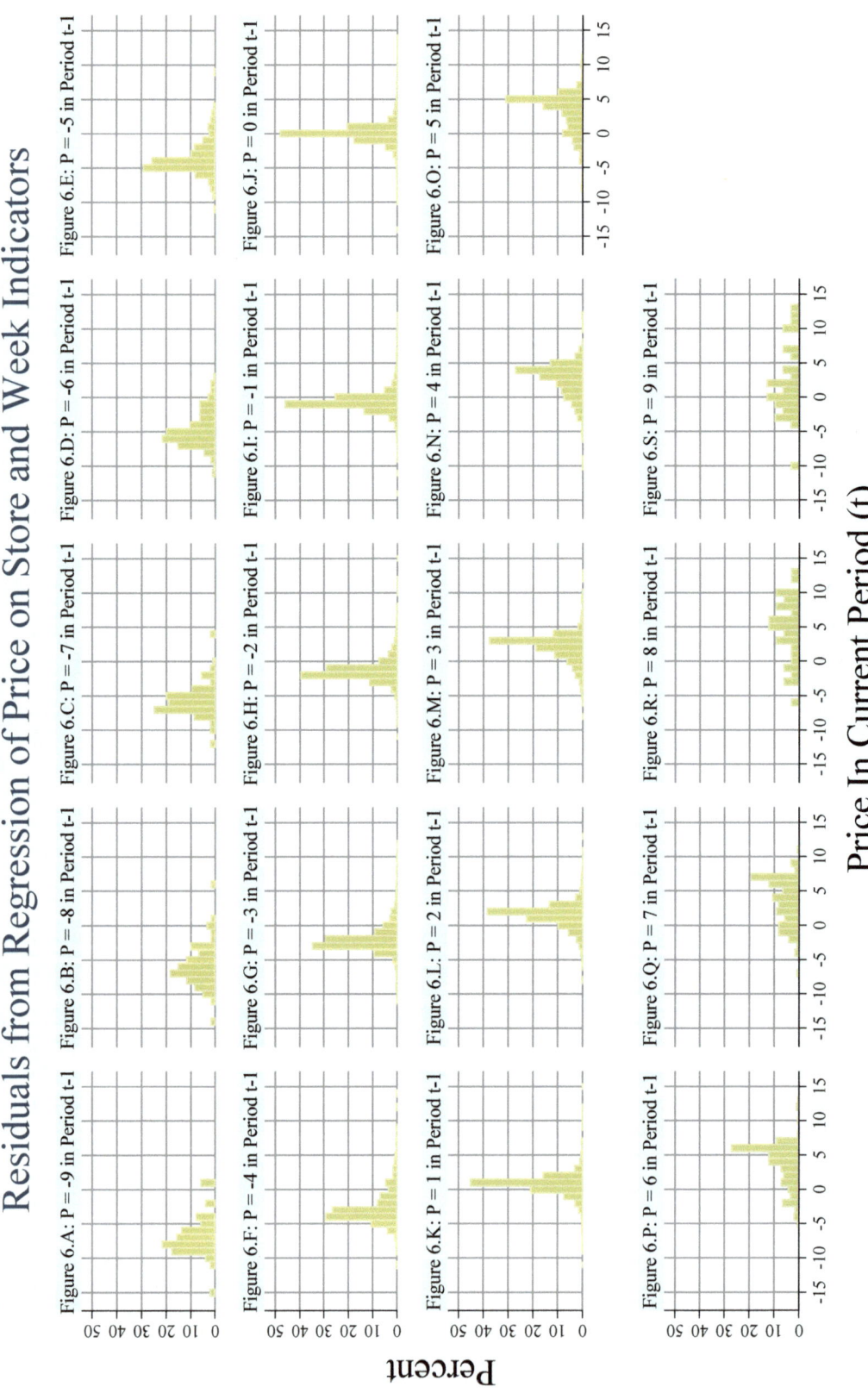

Figure 6: Single-Period Empirical Markov Transition Matrix
Relative Price in Current Week Conditional on Relative Price In Previous Week
Residuals from Regression of Price on Store and Week Indicators

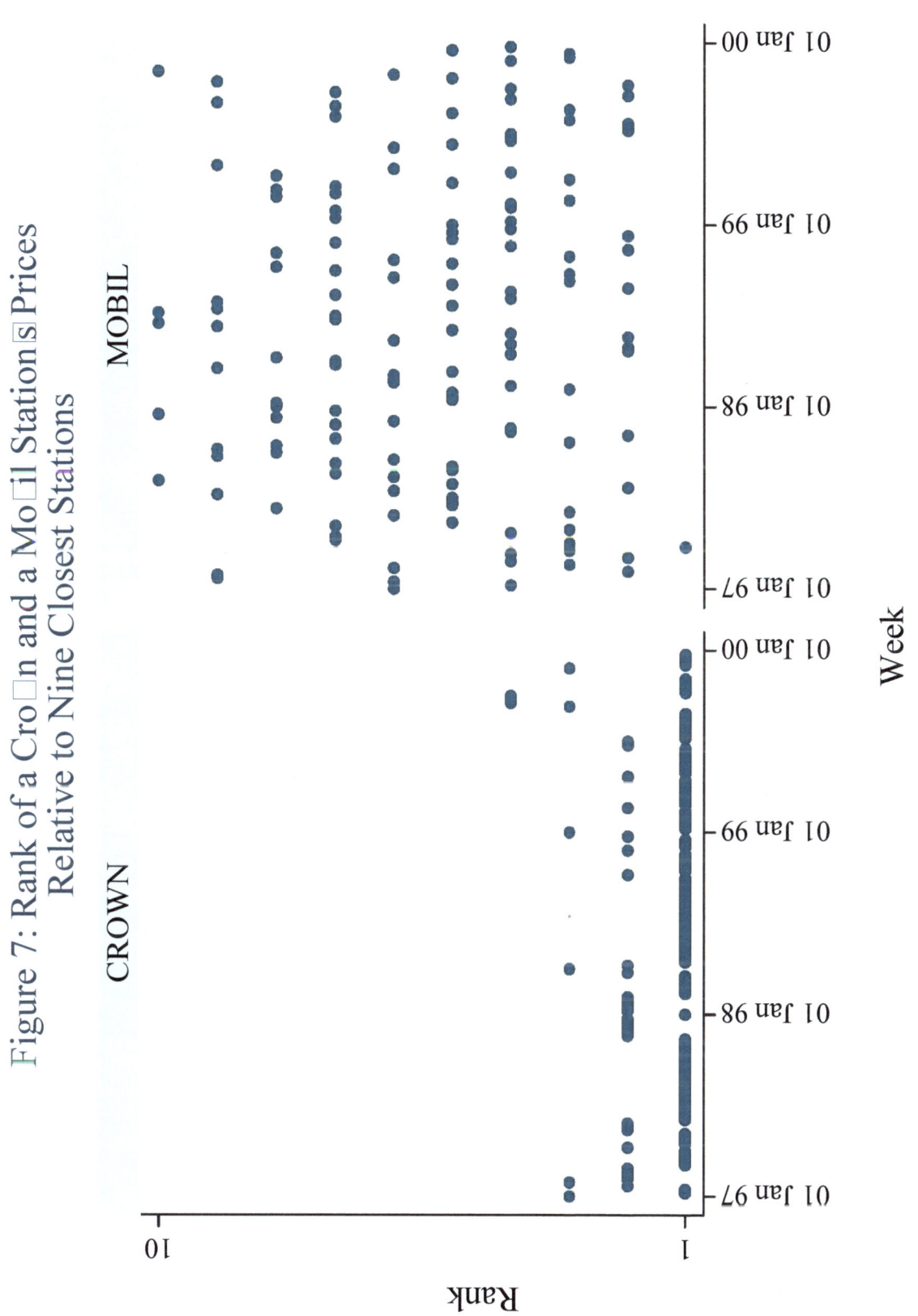

Figure 7: Rank of a Crown and a Mobil Station's Prices Relative to Nine Closest Stations

Figure 8: Markov Probabilities for Ten Closest Stations: Rank in Pricing Distribution at t conditional on Rank at t-1
1 Lowest 10 Highest

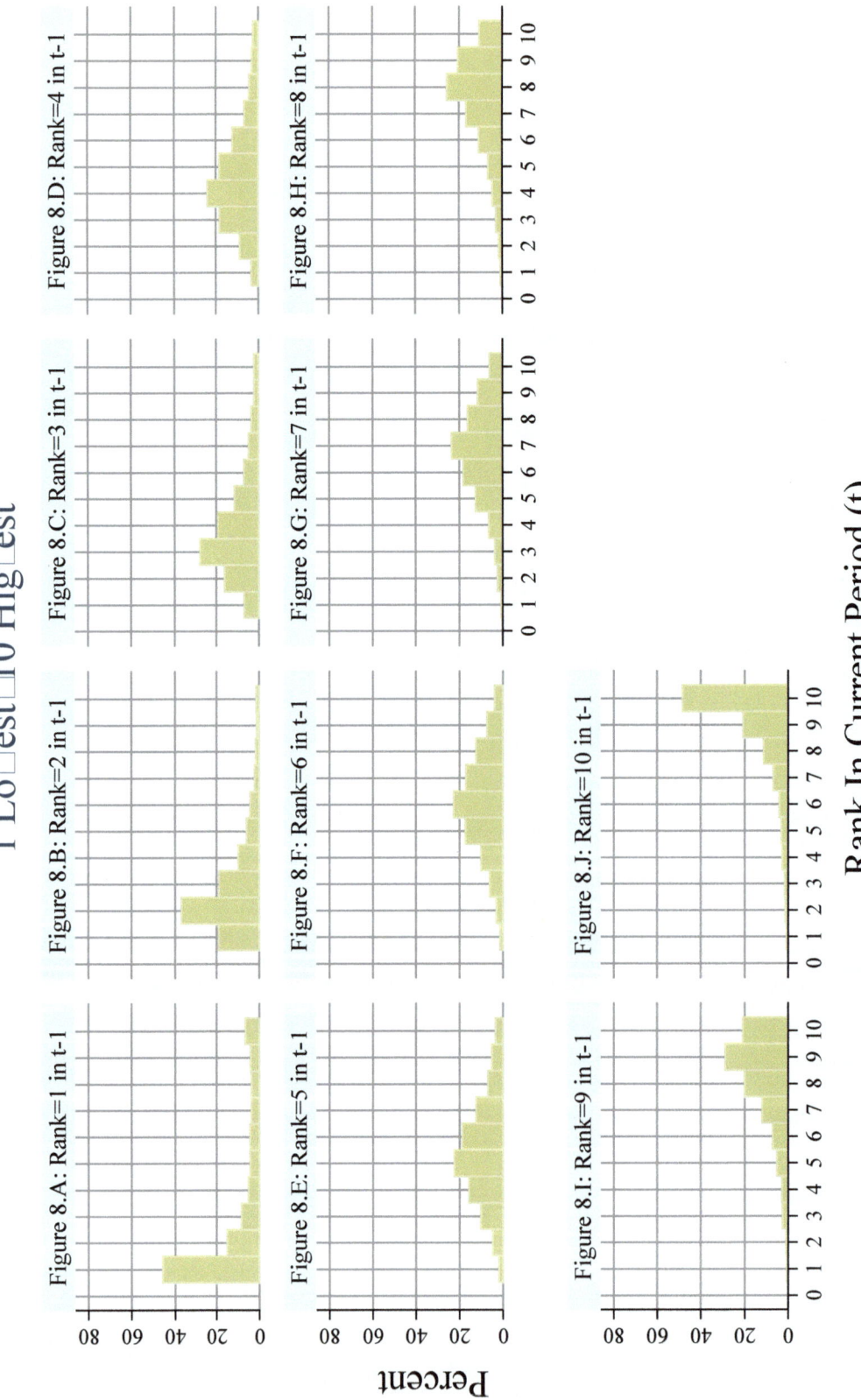

Rank In Current Period (t)

Figure 9: Markov Probabilities for Five Closest Stations: Rank in Pricing Distribution at t conditional on Rank at t-1

1 Lowest 5 Highest

Figure 9.A: Rank=1 in t-1

Figure 9.B: Rank=2 in t-1

Figure 9.C: Rank=3 in t-1

Figure 9.D: Rank=4 in t-1

Figure 9.E: Rank=5 in t-1

Percent

Rank In Current Period (t)

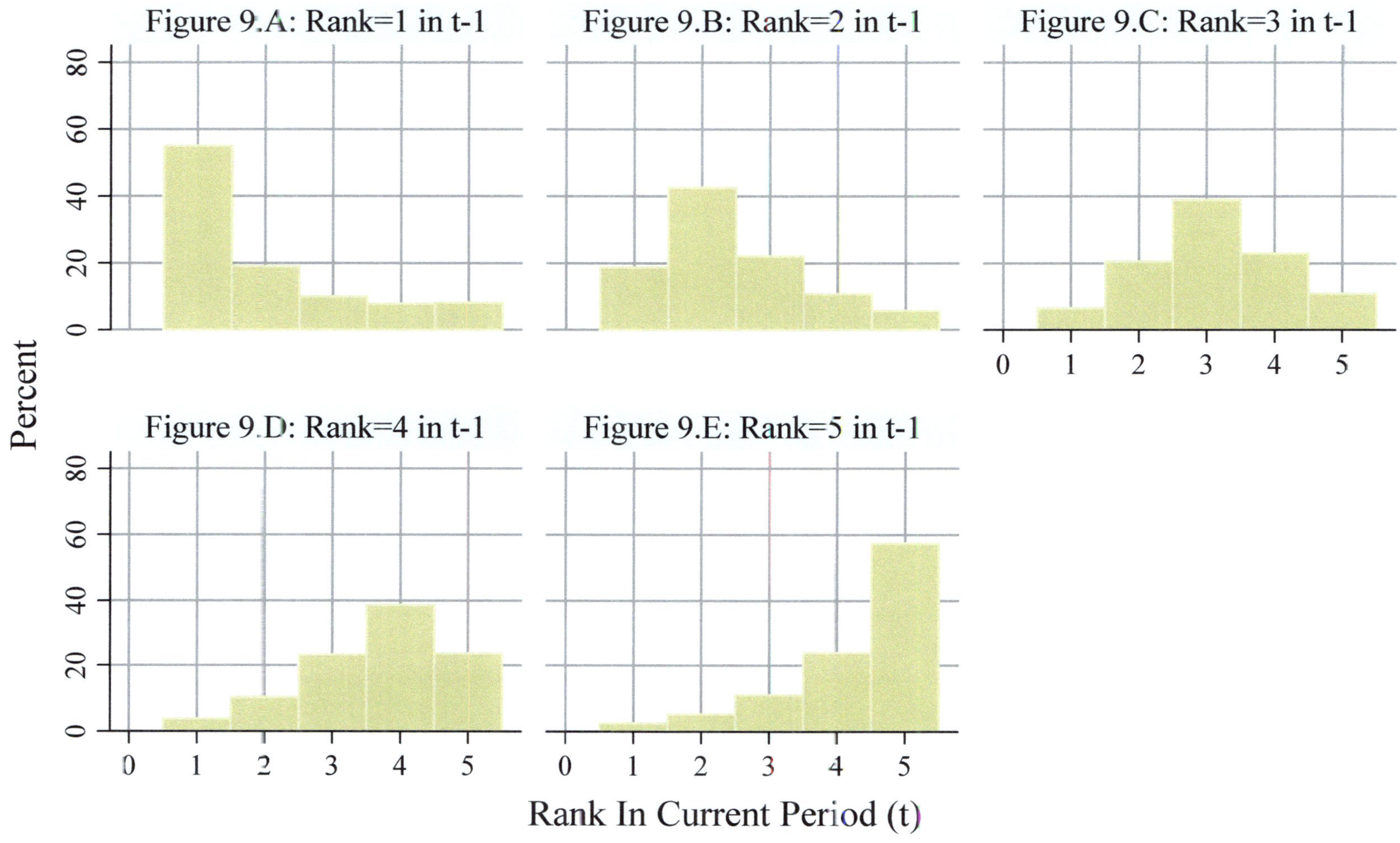

Appendix Table 1: Single-Period Empirical Markov Transition Matrix
Residuals from Regression of Price on Week Indicators
(Elements of Table are Percentages)

Relative Price at t-1	Relative Price at t																														
	-15	-14	-13	-12	-11	-10	-9	-8	-7	-6	-5	-4	-3	-2	-1	0	1	2	3	4	5	6	7	8	9	10	11	12	13	14	15
-9	1	0	2	2	5	17	32	18	9	5	3	3	1	1	1	0	1	1	1	0	0	0	0	0	0	0	0	0	0	0	0
-8	2	0	2	1	1	4	16	32	22	9	5	3	3	1	0	0	0	1	0	0	0	0	0	0	0	1	0	0	0	0	0
-7	1	0	0	0	1	1	5	11	37	25	8	3	3	2	2	1	0	0	0	0	0	0	0	0	0	0	0	0	0	0	0
-6	1	0	0	0	0	0	1	3	11	47	23	6	3	1	1	1	0	0	0	0	0	0	0	0	0	0	0	0	0	0	0
-5	0	0	0	0	0	0	1	1	3	15	44	23	7	2	2	1	0	0	0	0	0	0	0	0	0	0	0	0	0	0	0
-4	0	0	0	0	0	0	0	1	1	4	15	44	24	5	2	1	1	1	0	0	0	0	0	0	0	0	0	0	0	0	0
-3	0	0	0	0	0	0	0	0	1	1	4	16	45	21	5	3	1	1	1	0	0	0	0	0	0	0	0	0	0	0	0
-2	0	0	0	0	0	0	0	0	0	1	1	4	14	42	26	6	3	1	1	1	0	0	0	0	0	0	0	0	0	0	0
-1	0	0	0	0	0	0	0	0	0	0	0	2	4	14	42	24	6	3	1	1	1	0	0	0	0	0	0	0	0	0	0
0	0	0	0	0	0	0	0	0	0	0	0	0	2	4	13	47	24	4	2	1	0	0	0	0	0	0	0	0	0	0	0
1	0	0	0	0	0	0	0	0	0	0	0	0	1	1	4	17	49	19	4	2	1	1	1	0	0	0	0	0	0	0	0
2	0	0	0	0	0	0	0	0	0	0	0	0	0	1	3	7	18	44	18	4	2	1	1	0	0	0	0	0	0	0	0
3	0	0	0	0	0	0	0	0	0	0	0	0	0	1	2	4	7	18	46	13	4	1	1	1	0	0	0	0	0	0	0
4	0	0	0	0	0	0	0	0	0	0	0	0	0	0	1	3	7	10	19	37	13	4	1	1	1	0	0	0	0	0	0
5	0	0	0	0	0	0	0	0	0	0	0	0	1	1	2	4	4	9	11	17	34	11	2	1	1	1	1	0	0	0	0
6	0	0	0	0	0	0	0	0	0	0	0	0	0	1	2	2	6	9	12	11	16	25	10	4	1	0	0	0	0	0	0
7	0	0	0	0	0	0	0	0	0	0	0	0	1	1	2	2	6	9	12	8	11	10	25	7	2	1	1	0	1	0	0
8	0	0	0	0	0	0	0	0	0	0	0	1	1	3	1	4	6	5	8	6	8	14	7	17	12	5	1	1	1	1	0
9	0	0	0	0	0	0	0	0	0	0	0	0	0	2	1	2	11	6	5	10	7	8	10	3	19	9	4	2	1	0	1

Appendix Table 2: Single-Period Empirical Markov Transition Matrix
Residuals from Regression of Price on Store and Week Indicators
(Elements of Table Are Percentages)

Relative Price at t

Relative Price at t-1	-15	-14	-13	-12	-11	-10	-9	-8	-7	-6	-5	-4	-3	-2	-1	0	1	2	3	4	5	6	7	8	9	10	11	12	13	14	15
-9	2	0	0	0	2	4	18	22	16	14	6	8	0	4	0	0	6	0	0	0	0	0	0	0	0	0	0	0	0	0	0
-8	0	2	0	0	2	5	8	12	18	15	12	7	10	2	2	3	2	0	0	0	0	2	0	0	0	0	0	0	0	0	0
-7	0	0	0	2	0	2	2	9	25	19	20	10	2	6	2	1	0	0	0	2	0	0	0	0	0	0	0	0	0	0	0
-6	0	0	0	0	1	1	2	5	15	21	20	10	6	6	6	3	2	2	1	0	0	0	0	0	0	0	0	0	0	0	0
-5	0	0	0	0	0	0	1	2	3	8	29	26	10	8	5	2	3	2	1	1	1	0	0	0	0	0	0	0	0	0	0
-4	0	0	0	0	0	0	0	0	1	4	11	29	26	8	7	3	5	2	1	1	1	0	0	0	0	0	0	0	0	0	0
-3	0	0	0	0	0	0	0	0	0	1	2	9	35	29	9	6	3	2	1	1	0	0	0	0	0	0	0	0	0	0	0
-2	0	0	0	0	0	0	0	0	0	0	1	2	11	40	29	8	4	2	1	1	0	0	0	0	0	0	0	0	0	0	0
-1	0	0	0	0	0	0	0	0	0	0	0	1	3	13	46	25	5	2	1	1	0	0	0	0	0	0	0	0	0	0	0
0	0	0	0	0	0	0	0	0	0	0	0	1	2	5	18	48	20	4	1	0	0	0	0	0	0	0	0	0	0	0	0
1	0	0	0	0	0	0	0	0	0	0	0	0	2	3	7	21	45	16	3	1	1	0	0	0	0	0	0	0	0	0	0
2	0	0	0	0	0	0	0	0	0	0	0	1	1	3	6	10	23	38	13	3	1	1	0	0	0	0	0	0	0	0	0
3	0	0	0	0	0	0	0	0	0	0	0	1	1	3	4	6	11	19	38	12	2	1	1	0	0	0	0	0	0	0	0
4	0	0	0	0	0	0	0	0	0	0	0	0	2	3	4	7	8	11	17	27	13	3	1	0	0	0	0	0	0	0	0
5	0	0	0	0	0	0	0	1	0	0	0	1	3	4	8	6	6	8	16	31	10	2	1	0	1	1	0	0	0	0	0
6	0	0	0	0	0	0	0	0	0	0	0	2	1	7	3	4	7	6	7	12	12	27	9	0	0	0	1	0	0	0	0
7	0	0	0	0	0	0	0	0	1	0	0	2	1	4	8	8	6	9	8	10	6	12	19	2	3	0	1	0	0	0	0
8	0	0	0	0	0	0	0	0	0	3	0	0	6	3	6	3	3	3	9	6	12	12	3	9	6	9	0	3	3	0	0
9	0	0	0	0	0	3	0	0	0	0	0	3	10	6	10	13	6	13	3	6	0	3	6	0	0	6	3	3	3	0	0

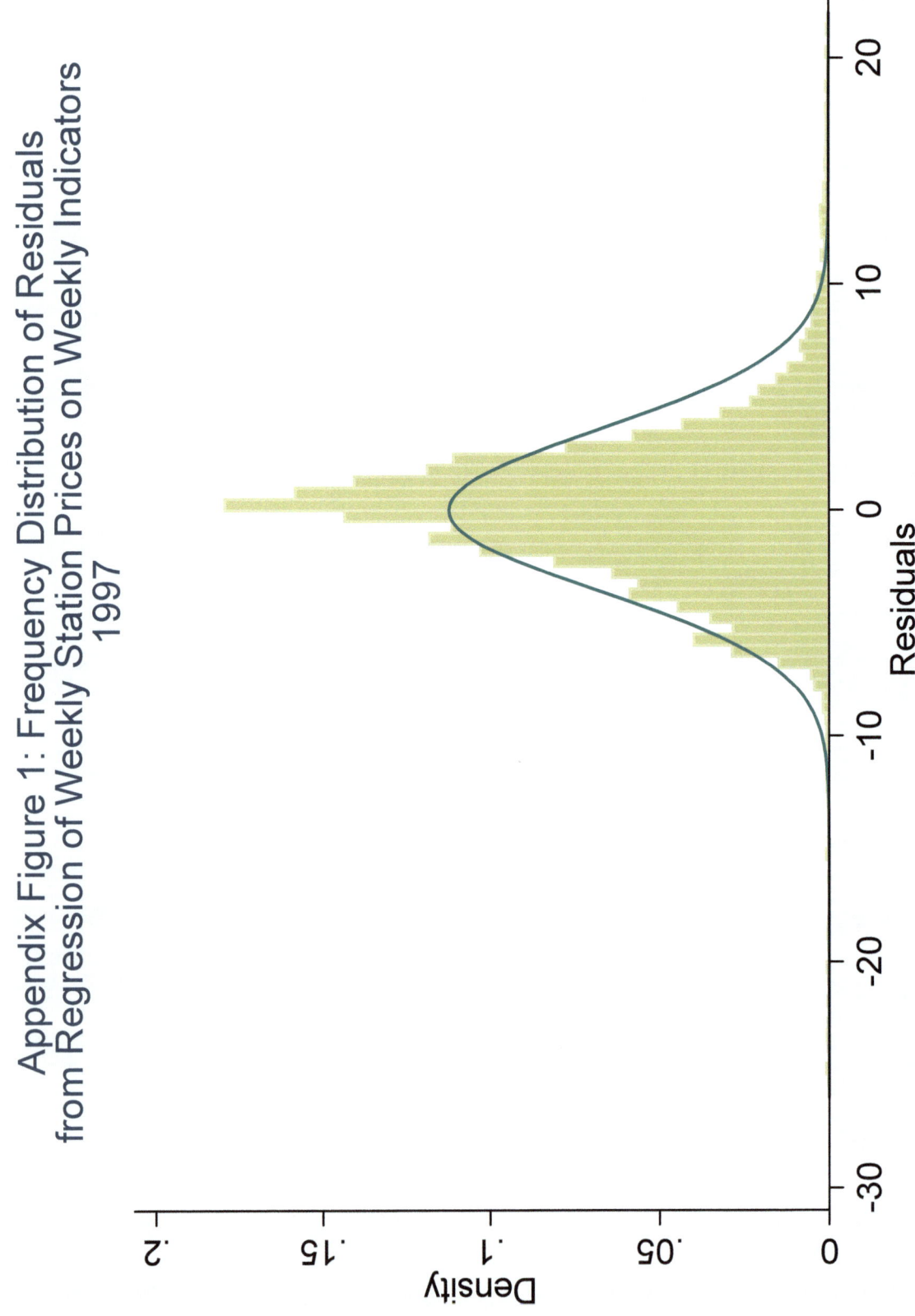

Appendix Figure 1: Frequency Distribution of Residuals
from Regression of Weekly Station Prices on Weekly Indicators
1997

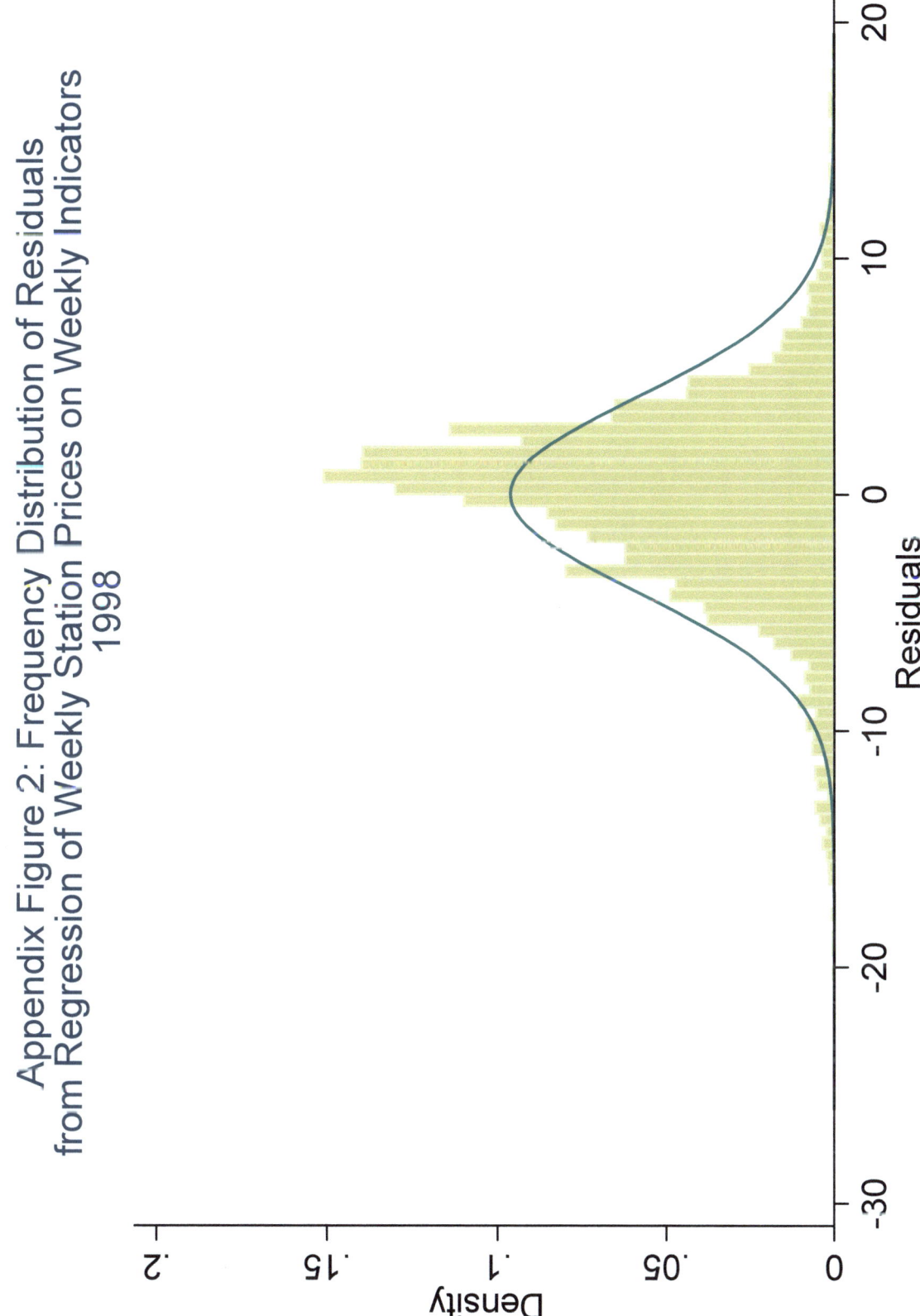

Appendix Figure 2: Frequency Distribution of Residuals from Regression of Weekly Station Prices on Weekly Indicators 1998

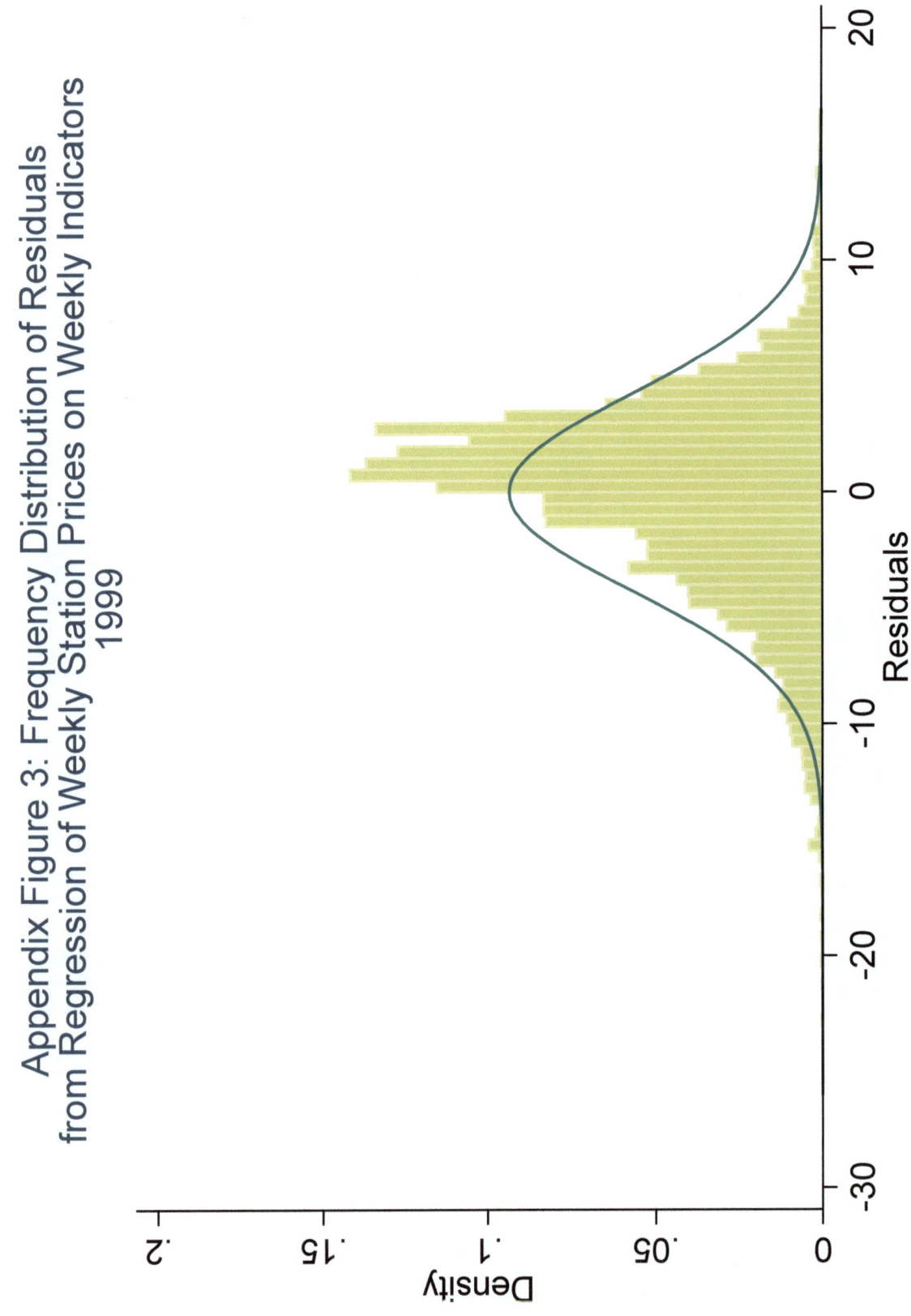

Appendix Figure 3: Frequency Distribution of Residuals from Regression of Weekly Station Prices on Weekly Indicators 1999

www.ingramcontent.com/pod-product-compliance
Lightning Source LLC
Chambersburg PA
CBHW050802180526
45159CB00004B/1517